Heinrich Böll
Irish Journal

Translated from the German by Leila Vennewitz

T M P

THE MARLBORO PRESS | NORTHWESTERN
Evanston, Illinois

The Marlboro Press/Northwestern
Northwestern University Press
Evanston, Illinois 60208-4210

Originally published in German under the title *Irisches Tagebuch.* Copyright © 1957 by Kiepenheuer & Witsch, Cologne-Berlin. English translation copyright © 1967 by Leila Vennewitz. Northwestern University Press edition published 1994 by arrangement with Kiepenheuer & Witsch and Leila Vennewitz. The Marlboro Press/Northwestern edition published 1998. All rights reserved.

Printed in the United States of America

ISBN 0-8101-6062-5

Library of Congress Cataloging-in-Publication Data

Böll, Heinrich, 1917–
    [Irisches Tagebuch. English]
    Irish journal / Heinrich Böll ; translated from the German by Leila Vennewitz.
        p. cm. — (Marlboro travel)
    Originally published: Evanston, Ill. : Northwestern University Press, 1994.
    ISBN 0-8101-6062-5 (alk. paper)
    1. Ireland—Description and travel. 2. Böll, Heinrich, 1917– —Journeys—Ireland. I. Vennewitz, Leila. II. Title. III. Series.
DA978.B5613 1998
914.1'504'823—dc21   98-6903
                                                               CIP

The paper used in this publication meets the minimum requirements of the American National Standard for Information Sciences—Permanence of Paper for Printed Library Materials, ANSI Z39.48-1984.

Irish Journal

Translator's Acknowledgment

I am deeply grateful to my husband, William Vennewitz, for his assistance in this translation.

Lelia Vennewitz
Vancouver, Canada

This Ireland exists: but whoever goes there and fails to find it has no claim on the author.

I dedicate this little book to the man who encouraged me to write it: Karl Korn.

H. B.

The Ireland described in this book is that of the mid-1950s. My comments on the great changes that have taken place in that country since then are contained in the Epilogue.

Heinrich Böll

1. Arrival I

As soon as I boarded the steamer I could see, hear, and smell that I had crossed a frontier. I had seen one of England's gentle, lovely sides: Kent, almost bucolic—I had barely skimmed the topographical marvel that is London —then seen one of England's gloomier sides, Liverpool —but here on the steamer there was no more England: here there was already a smell of peat, the sound of throaty Celtic from between decks and the bar, here Europe's social order was already assuming new forms: poverty was no longer "no disgrace," it was neither honor nor disgrace: it was—as an element of social awareness—as irrelevant as wealth; trouser creases had lost their sharp edge, and the safety pin, that ancient Celtic clasp, had come into its own again. Where the button had looked like a full stop, put there by the tailor, the safety pin had been hung on like a comma; a sign of improvisation, it draped the material in folds, where the button had prevented this. I also saw it used to attach price tickets, lengthen suspenders, replace cuff-links, finally used as a weapon by a small boy to pierce a man's trouser seat: the boy was surprised, frightened because the man did not react in any way; the boy carefully tapped the man with his forefinger to see if he was still alive: he was still alive, and patted the boy laughingly on the shoulder.

Longer and longer grew the line-up at the counter

where the nectar of Western Europe was available in generous quantities for a small sum: tea, as if the Irish were doing their utmost not to surrender this world record held by them just ahead of England: almost ten pounds of tea are consumed annually per head in Ireland; enough tea to fill a small swimming pool must flow down every Irish throat every year.

As I slowly moved along in the line-up I had time to recall the other Irish world records: this little country holds not only the tea-drinking record, but also the one for the consecration of new priests (the Archdiocese of Cologne would have to consecrate nearly a thousand new priests a year to compete with a small archdiocese in Ireland); the third world record held by Ireland is that of moviegoing (again—how much in common despite the differences!—just ahead of England); finally the fourth, a significant one of which I dare not say it stands in causal relationship to the first three: in Ireland there are fewer suicides than anywhere else on earth. The records for whisky-drinking and cigarette-smoking have not yet been ascertained, but in these disciplines Ireland is also well ahead, this little country the size of Bavaria but with fewer inhabitants than those between Essen and Dortmund.

A cup of tea at midnight, while standing shivering in the west wind as the steamer pushes slowly out to the open sea—then a whisky upstairs in the bar, where the throaty Celtic was still to be heard, but from only one Irish throat now. In the room off the bar, nuns settled like great birds getting ready for the night, warm under their headdresses, their long habits, drawing in their long rosaries as ropes are drawn in when a boat leaves; a young man standing at the bar with a baby in his arms was refused a fifth glass of beer, his wife, who was standing beside him holding a little girl of two, also had her glass taken away by the bartender without a refill. The bar slowly emptied, the throaty Celtic was silent, the nuns' heads were gently nodding in sleep; one of them had forgotten to draw in her rosary, the plump beads rolled to and fro with the movement of the ship. Carrying their children, the couple who had been refused a drink swayed past me toward a corner where they had built themselves a little fort out of suitcases and cardboard boxes. Two more children were asleep over there, leaning on either side of their grandmother, whose black shawl seemed to offer warmth for three. The baby and its two-year-old sister were stowed away in a laundry basket and covered up; the parents crept silently in between two suitcases, their bodies pressed close together, and the man's thin white hand spread a raincoat over them like an awning. Silence; the suitcase locks clinked gently to the rhythm of the moving ship.

I had forgotten to get myself a place for the night. I clambered over legs, boxes, suitcases. Cigarettes glowed in the dark; I caught scraps of whispered conversation: "Connemara . . . no luck . . . waitress in London." I crouched between some lifeboats and lifebelts, but the west wind was keen and damp. I stood up, made my way across the ship, which one would have thought full of emigrants rather than homecomers—legs, glowing cigarettes, scraps of whispered conversation—till a priest grasped the bottom of my coat and with a smile invited me to sit down next to him. I leaned back to sleep, but to the right of the priest, under a green and gray striped

3

blanket, a light clear voice was speaking: "No, Father, no, no . . . it hurts too much to think of Ireland. Once a year I have to go there to visit my parents, and my grandmother is still alive. Do you know County Galway?"

"No," murmured the priest.

"Connemara?"

"No."

"You should go there, and don't forget on your way back in the port of Dublin to notice what's exported from Ireland: children and priests, nuns and biscuits, whisky and horses, beer and dogs. . . ."

"My child," said the priest gently, "you should not mention these things in the same breath."

A match flared under the green-gray blanket, a sharp profile was visible for a second or two.

"I don't believe in God," said the light clear voice, "no, I don't believe in God—so why shouldn't I mention priests and whisky, nuns and biscuits, in the same breath? I don't believe in *Kathleen ni Houlihan* either, that fairy-tale Ireland. . . . I was a waitress in London for two years: I've seen how many loose women. . . ."

"My child," said the priest in a low voice.

". . . how many loose women *Kathleen ni Houlihan* has sent to London, the isle of the saints."

"My child!"

"That's what the priest back home used to call me too: my child. He used to come on his bike, a long way, to read Mass to us on Sundays, but even he couldn't stop *Kathleen ni Houlihan* exporting her most precious possession: her children. Go to Connemara, Father—I'm sure you've never seen so much lovely scenery, with so

4

few people in it, all at once. Perhaps you can read Mass to us one Sunday, then you'll see me kneeling devoutly in church."

"I thought you didn't believe in God."

"But d'you suppose I could afford—or be so cruel to my parents—not to go to church? 'Our daughter is still the same devout, good girl, such a good daughter.' And my grandmother kisses me when I go home, blesses me and says: 'Stay as devout as you are, dear child!' . . . Do you know how many grandchildren my grandmother has?"

"My child, my child," said the priest gently.

The cigarette glowed sharply, revealing the severe profile for a second.

"My grandmother has thirty-six grandchildren, thirty-six. She used to have thirty-eight, one was shot down in the Battle of Britain, another one went down with a British submarine—there are thirty-six still alive; twenty in Ireland, the others. . . ."

"There are countries," said the priest in a low voice, "that export hygiene and suicide ideas, nuclear weapons, machine guns, automobiles. . . ."

"Oh I know," said the light, clear girlish voice, "I know all about that: I've a brother myself who is a priest, and two cousins, they're the only ones in the whole family who have cars."

"My child. . . ."

"I'm going to try and get some sleep now—goodnight, Father, goodnight."

The glowing cigarette flew over the railing, the green-gray blanket was pulled snugly around the slim shoulders, the priest's head shook rhythmically from side to side; but perhaps it was only the rhythm of the ship that was moving his head.

"My child," he said once more in a low voice, but there was no answer.

He leaned back with a sigh, turned up his coat collar; there were four safety pins on the underside as a reserve; four, hanging from a fifth that was stuck in at right angles, swinging from side to side in time with the gentle thrusts of the steamer as it headed into the gray darkness toward the isle of saints.

2. Arrival II

A cup of tea, at dawn, while standing shivering in the west wind, the isle of saints still hiding from the sun in the morning mist; here on this island, then, live the only people in Europe that never set out to conquer, although they were conquered several times, by Danes, Normans, Englishmen—all they sent out was priests, monks, missionaries who, by way of this strange detour via Ireland, brought the spirit of Thebaic asceticism to Europe; here, more than a thousand years ago, so far from the center of things, as if it had slipped way out into the Atlantic, lay the glowing heart of Europe. . . .

So many green-gray blankets drawn snugly around slim shoulders, so many sharp profiles, and on so many turned-up priests' collars the reserve safety pin stuck in at right angles with two, three, or four more pins dangling from it . . . thin faces, bleary eyes, in the laundry basket the baby drinking its bottle while at the tea counter the father was vainly struggling to get some beer. Slowly the morning sun picked white houses out of the mist, a lighthouse barked red-and-white toward the ship, slowly the steamer panted into the harbor of Dun Laoghaire. Seagulls greeted it, the gray silhouette of Dublin became visible, vanished again; churches, monuments, docks, a gasometer: tentative wisps of smoke from a few fireplaces: breakfast time, but only for a few: Ireland was still asleep, porters down on the dock

7

rubbed the sleep from their eyes, taxi drivers shivered in the morning wind. Irish tears greeted home and the homecomers. Names were tossed back and forth like balls.

I staggered wearily from the ship into the train, and a few minutes later from the train into the great dark railway station of Westland Row, from there onto the street: a young woman was just lifting an orange milk jug into the room from the window sill of a black house; she smiled at me, and I smiled back.

Now I had no idea, although I soon began to suspect, that the hours between seven and ten in the morning are the only ones during which the Irish incline toward taciturnity, for whoever I asked, and whatever I asked about, I received the brief answer: "Sorry." Like the German apprentice in Amsterdam in the old tale who supposed that everything he asked about belonged to Mr. Kannitverstan, since that was the only word he ever heard in answer to his questions, so I would have liked to ask: Who owns the big ships in the harbor? "Sorry." Who is that standing up there all by himself in the morning mist on a pedestal? "Sorry." Who do these ragged, barefoot children belong to? "Sorry." Who is this mysterious young man standing on the back platform of the bus so skillfully imitating a machine gun—tok tok tok tok? "Sorry." And who is that riding by with his crop and his gray top hat? "Sorry." But I decided not to try and apply my meager knowledge of the language and to rely more on my eyes than my tongue or the ears of other people, and to study the shop signs instead. And there they all came rushing to meet me as bookkeepers, innkeepers, greengrocers—Joyce and Yeats, McCarthy and Molloy, O'Neill and O'Connor, even Jackie Coogan's footsteps seemed to lead here, and I was forced to admit that the man up there on the pedestal, still looking so forlorn in the chill of the morning, was of course not Mr. Sorry but Nelson.

I bought a paper, something called *The Irish Digest*, and, drawn by a sign promising "Bed and Breakfast Reasonable," decided on a reasonable breakfast.

If Continental tea is like a faded yellow telegraph form, in these islands to the west of Ostend it has the dark, glimmering tones of Russian icons, before the milk gives it a color similar to the complexion of an overfed baby; on the Continent weak tea is served in fragile porcelain, here it is casually poured into thick earthenware cups from battered metal teapots, a heavenly brew to restore the traveler, dirt cheap too.

The breakfast was good, the tea worthy of renown, and thrown in for free was the smile of the young Irish girl who served it.

I glanced through the paper and the first thing I saw was a letter demanding that Nelson be brought down from his high perch and replaced by a statue of the Virgin Mary. Another letter demanding Nelson's downfall, then another. . . .

It was now eight o'clock, tongues were loosened, I was engulfed in words of which I only understood one: Germany. I decided to strike back, in friendly but determined fashion, with the weapon of the country, "Sorry," and to enjoy the free smiles of the tousled tea goddess, when a sudden roar, a sound almost like thunder, startled me. Could there be so many trains on this strange island? The thunder continued, became articu-

9

late, the powerful opening bars of the *Tantum ergo* beginning with *Sacramentum—veneremur cernui* became distinguishable, and sung clear and true to the last syllable it pealed out over Westland Row from St. Andrew's Church opposite, and just as the first cups of tea were as good as all the others I would drink—in desolate, dirty little hamlets, in hotels and by firesides—so I was left with the impression of an overwhelming piety as it flooded Westland Row after the *Tantum ergo:* in Germany you would only see that many people coming out of church after Easter Mass or at Christmas; but I had not forgotten the confession of the unbeliever with the sharp profile.

It was still only eight in the morning, Sunday, too early to wake my host: but the tea was cold, the café smelled of mutton fat, the customers were gathering up their boxes and suitcases and heading for their buses. Listlessly I turned the pages of *The Irish Digest*, haltingly translated the beginnings of some articles and short stories till a one-line aphorism on page 23 caught my eye: I understood it long before I would have been able to translate it: untranslated, not in German and yet understood, it was even more effective than if it had been rendered into German: *The cemeteries*, it said, *are full of people the world could not do without.*

This wisdom seemed to me to be worth a trip to Dublin, and I made up my mind to lock it securely in my heart for the moments when I would be feeling my importance (later on it seemed to me a kind of key to this strange mixture of passion and equability, to that temperamental weariness, that indifference coupled with fanaticism, which I was to encounter so often).

Great cool private houses lay hidden behind rhododendrons, behind palm trees and oleander bushes, when I had decided to wake my host despite the barbarically early hour: mountains became visible in the background, long rows of trees.

Eight hours later a German compatriot was declaring categorically to me: "Everything here is dirty, everything is expensive, and nowhere can you get a proper châteaubriand," and already I was defending Ireland, although I had only been in the country ten hours, ten hours out of which I had slept for five, bathed for one, spent one in church, argued for one with my compatriot, who could pit six months against my ten hours. I defended Ireland passionately, fought with tea, *Tantum ergo,* Joyce and Yeats against the châteaubriand, which was particularly dangerous for me since I didn't know what it was (it was not till long after I got home that I had to look it up to identify it: a kind of steak, it said), I just sensed dimly, as I fought it, that it must be a meat dish—but my struggle was in vain; the man going abroad would like to forego the disadvantages of his native land—all that rushing about at home!—but take his châteaubriand with him; probably one cannot drink tea in Rome with impunity, any more than one can drink coffee in Ireland with impunity, except perhaps in the home of an Italian. I gave up the struggle, drove back in the bus, and marveled at the endless line-ups in front of the movies, of which there seemed to be plenty: in the morning, I thought, they crowd into and around the churches, and in the evening apparently into and around the movies; at a green newsstand I fell victim again to the smile of an Irish girl, bought newspapers, cigarettes, chocolate, then my eye fell on a book lying unnoticed among pamphlets: its white cover, bordered in red, was already soiled; secondhand, I could have it for a shilling, and I bought it. It was Goncharov's *Oblomov*, translated into English. Although I knew Oblomov's home to be some two or three thousand miles farther east, I suspected that he was not out of place in this country, where everyone hates to get up early in the morning.

3. Pray for the Soul of Michael O'Neill

At Swift's tomb my heart had caught a chill, so clean was St. Patrick's Cathedral, so empty of people and so full of patriotic marble figures, so deep under the cold stone did the desperate Dean seem to lie, Stella beside him: two square brass plates, burnished as if by the hand of a German housewife: the larger one for Swift, the smaller for Stella; I wished I had some thistles, hard, big, long-stemmed, a few clover leaves, and some thornless, gentle blossoms, jasmine perhaps or honeysuckle; that would have been the right thing to offer these two, but my hands were as empty as the church, just as cold and just as clean. Regimental banners hung side by side, half-lowered: did they really smell of gunpowder? They looked as if they did, but the only smell was of mold, as in every church where for centuries no incense has been burned; I felt as though I were being bombarded with needles of ice; I fled, and it was only in the entrance that I saw there was someone in the church after all: the cleaningwoman; she was washing down the porch with lye, cleaning what was already clean enough.

In front of the cathedral stood an Irish beggar, the first I had met: beggars like this one are only to be found otherwise in southern countries, but in the south the sun shines: here, north of the 53rd parallel, rags and tatters are something different from south of the 30th parallel; rain falls on poverty, and here even an incorrigible esthete could no longer regard dirt as picturesque; in the slums around St. Patrick's, squalor still huddles in many a corner, many a house, exactly as Swift must have seen it in 1743.

Both the beggar's coatsleeves hung empty at his sides; these coverings for limbs he no longer possessed were dirty; epileptic twitching ran like lightning across his face, and yet his thin, dark face had a beauty that will be noted in a book other than mine. I had to light his cigarette for him and place it between his lips; I had to put money for him in his coat pocket: I almost felt as if I were furnishing a corpse with money. Darkness hung over Dublin: every shade of gray between black and white had found its own little cloud, the sky was covered with a plumage of innumerable grays: not a streak, not a scrap of Irish green; slowly, twitching, the beggar from St. Patrick's Park crossed over under this sky into the slums.

In the slums dirt sometimes lies in black flakes on the windowpanes, as if thrown there on purpose, fished up from fireplaces, from canals; but things don't happen here so easily on purpose, and not much happens by itself: drink happens here, love, prayer, and cursing. God is passionately loved and no doubt equally passionately hated.

In the dark back yards, the ones Swift's eyes saw, this dirt has been piled up in decades and centuries: the depressing sediment of time. In the windows of the secondhand shops lay a confused variety of junk, and at last I found one of the objects of my journey: the private drinking booth with the leather curtain; here the drinker locks himself in like a horse; to be alone with whisky and pain, with belief and unbelief, he lowers himself deep below the surface of time, into the caisson of passivity, as long as his money lasts; till he is compelled to float up again to the surface of time, to take part somehow in the weary paddling: meaningless, helpless movements, since every vessel is destined to drift toward the dark waters of the Styx. No wonder there is no room in these pubs for women, the busy ones of this earth: here the man is alone with his whisky, far removed from all the activities in which he has been forced to participate, activities known as family, occupation, honor, society; the whisky is bitter, comforting, and somewhere to the west, across three thousand miles of water, and somewhere to the east, two seas to cross to get there—are those who believe in activity and progress. Yes, they exist, such people; how bitter the whisky is, how comforting; the beefy innkeeper passes the next glass into the booth. His eyes are sober, blue: he believes in what those who make him rich do not believe in. In the woodwork of the pub, the paneled walls of the private drinking booth, lurk jokes and curses, hopes and prayers of other people; how many, I wonder?

Already the caisson—the booth—can be felt sinking deeper and deeper toward the dark bottom of time: past wrecks, past fish, but even down here there is no peace now that the deep-sea divers have invented their instruments. Float up again, then, take a deep breath, and plunge once more into activities, the kind called honor, occupation, family, society, before the caisson is pried open by the deep-sea divers. "How much?" Coins, many coins, thrown into the hard blue eyes of the innkeeper.

The sky was still feathered with manifold grays, not a sign of the countless Irish greens, as I made my way to the other church. Not much time had passed: the beggar was standing in the church doorway, and the cigarette I had placed between his lips was just being taken out of his mouth by schoolboys, the end nipped off with care so as not to lose a single crumb of tobacco, the butt placed carefully in the beggar's coat pocket, his cap removed—who, even when he has lost both arms, would enter the house of God with his cap on his head?—the door was held open for him, the empty coatsleeves slapped against the doorposts: they were wet and dirty, as if he had dragged them through the gutter, but inside no one is bothered by dirt.

St. Patrick's Cathedral had been so empty, so clean, and so beautiful; this church was full of people, full of cheap sentimental decoration, and although it wasn't exactly dirty it was messy: the way a living room looks in a family where there are a lot of children. Some people—I heard that one was a German who thus spreads the blessings of German culture throughout Ireland—must make a fortune in Ireland with plaster figures, but anger at the maker of this junk pales at the sight of those who pray in front of his products: the more highly colored, the better; the more sentimental, the better: "as lifelike as possible" (watch out, you who are praying, for life is not "lifelike").

A dark-haired beauty, defiant-looking as an offended angel, prays before the statue of St. Magdalene; her face has a greenish pallor: her thoughts and prayers are written down in the book which I do not know. Schoolboys with hurling sticks under their arms pray at the Stations

16

of the Cross; tiny oil lamps burn in dark corners in front of the Sacred Heart, the Little Flower, St. Anthony, St. Francis; here religion is savored to the last drop; the beggar sits in the last row, his twitching face turned toward the space where incense clouds still hang.

New and remarkable achievements of the devotional industry are the neon halo around Mary's head and the phosphorescent cross in the stoup, glowing rosily in the twilight of the church. Will there be separate entries in the book for those who prayed in front of this trash and those who prayed in Italy in front of Fra Angelico's frescoes?

The black-haired beauty with the greenish pallor is still staring at Magdalene, the beggar's face is still twitching; his whole body is convulsed, the convulsions make the coins in his pocket tinkle softly; the boys with the hurling sticks seem to know the beggar, they seem to understand the twitching of his face, the low babble: one of them puts his hand into the beggar's pocket, and on the boy's grubby palm lie four coins: two pennies, a sixpence, and a threepenny bit. One penny and the threepenny bit remain on the boy's palm, the rest tinkles into the offering box; here lie the frontiers of mathematics, psychology and political economy, the frontiers of all the more or less exact sciences crisscross each other in the twitching of the beggar's epileptic face: a foundation too narrow for me to trust myself to it. But the cold from Swift's tomb still clings to my heart: cleanliness, emptiness, marble figures, regimental banners, and the woman who was cleaning what was clean enough; St. Patrick's Cathedral was beautiful, this church is ugly, but it is used, and I found on its benches something I found on many Irish church benches: little enamel plaques requesting a prayer: "Pray for the soul of Michael O'Neill, who died 17.1.1933 at the age of sixty. Pray for the soul of Mary Keegan, who died on May 9, 1945, at the age of eighteen"; what a pious, cunning blackmail; the dead come alive again, their date of death is linked in the mind of the one reading the plaque with his own experience that day, that month, that year. With twitching face Hitler was waiting to seize power when sixty-year-old Michael O'Neill died here; when Germany capitulated, eighteen-year-old Mary Keegan was dying. "Pray"—I read—"for Kevin Cassidy, who died 20.12.1930 at the age of thirteen," and a shock went through me like an electric current, for in December 1930 I had been thirteen myself: in a great dark apartment in south Cologne—residential apartment house, is what it would have been called in 1908—I sat clutching my Christmas report; vacation had begun, and through a worn place in the cinnamon-colored drapes I looked down onto the wintry street.

I saw the street colored reddish-brown, as if smeared with unreal, stage blood: the piles of snow were red, the sky over the city was red, and the screech of the street-car as it swerved into the loop of the terminus, even this screech I heard as red. But when I pushed my face through the slit between the drapes I saw it as it really was: the edges of the snow islands were brown, the asphalt was black, the streetcar was the color of neglected teeth, but the grinding sound as the streetcar swerved into the loop, the grinding I heard as pale green —pale green as it shot piercingly up into the bare branches of the trees.

18

On that day Kevin Cassidy died in Dublin, thirteen years old, the same age as I was then: here the bier was set up, *Dies irae, dies illa* was sung from the organ loft. Kevin's frightened schoolmates filled the benches; incense, candle warmth, silver tassels on the black shroud, while I was folding up my report, getting my sled out from the closet to go tobogganing. I had a B in Latin, and Kevin's coffin was being lowered into the grave.

Later, when I had left the church and was walking along the streets, Kevin Cassidy was still beside me: I saw him alive, as old as I was, saw myself for a few moments as a thirty-seven-year-old Kevin: father of three children, living in the slums around St. Patrick's; the whisky was bitter, cool, and costly, from Swift's tomb ice needles came shooting out at him: his dark-haired wife's face had a greenish pallor, he had debts and a little house like countless others in London, thousands in Dublin, modest, two-storied, poor; petty bourgeois, stuffy, depressing, is what the incorrigible esthete would call it (but watch out, esthete: in one of these houses James Joyce was born, in another Sean O'Casey).

So close was Kevin's shadow that I ordered two whiskies when I returned to the private drinking booth, but the shadow did not raise the glass to its lips, and so I drank for Kevin Cassidy, who died 20.12.1930 at the age of thirteen—I drank for him too.

4. Mayo – God Help Us

In the center of Ireland, in Athlone, two and a half hours by express from Dublin, the train is split up into two. The better half, the one with the dining car, goes on to Galway; the underprivileged half, the one we remain in, goes to Westport. We would be watching the departure of the dining car, where lunch was just being served, with even more painful emotions if we had any money, English or Irish, to pay for breakfast or lunch. But as it happens, since there was only half an hour between the arrival of the ship and the departure of the train and the exchange bureaus in Dublin do not open until 9:30, all we have is flimsy notes, useless here, just as they come from the printing presses of the German Federal Bank, and central Ireland knows no rate for these.

I still have not quite got over the scare I had in Dublin: when I left the station to look for a place to change some money, I was almost run over by a bright-red panel truck whose sole decoration was a big swastika. Had someone sold *Völkischer Beobachter* delivery trucks here, or did the *Völkischer Beobachter* still have a branch office here? This one looked exactly like those I remembered; but the driver crossed himself as he smilingly signaled to me to proceed, and on closer inspection I saw what had happened. It was simply the "Swastika Laundry," which had painted the year of its founding, 1912, clearly beneath the swastika; but the mere possibility that it might have been one of those others was enough to take my breath away.

I could not find a bank open and returned discouraged to the station, having already decided to let the train for Westport leave as I could not pay for the tickets. We had the choice of taking a hotel room and waiting till the next day, till the next train (for the afternoon train would be too late for us to make our bus connection)— or in some way boarding the Westport train without tickets; this "some way" was found: we traveled on credit. The stationmaster in Dublin, touched by the spectacle of three tired children, two dejected women, and a helpless father (escaped only two minutes earlier from the swastika truck!), worked out that the night in the hotel would cost as much as the whole train journey to Westport: he wrote down my name, the *number of persons traveling on credit*, shook my hand reassuringly, and signaled to the train to leave.

So on this strange island we managed to enjoy the only kind of credit which we had never been given and never tried to obtain, the credit of a railway company.

But unfortunately there was no breakfast on credit in the dining car; the attempt to obtain it failed: the bank notes, in spite of the crisp new paper, did not convince the headwaiter. With a sigh we changed the last pound, had the Thermos flask filled with tea and ordered a package of sandwiches. The conductors were left with the stern duty of writing strange names down in their notebooks. It happened once, twice, three times, and the alarming question arose for us: shall we have to pay these unique debts once, twice, or three times?

The new conductor, who joined the train at Athlone,

had red hair and was eager and young; when I confessed to him that we had no tickets, a ray of recognition crossed his face. Clearly he had been told about us, clearly our names and our credit together with the *number of persons traveling on credit* had been telegraphed through from station to station.

For four hours after Athlone, the train, now a local one, wound its way through smaller and smaller stations farther and farther to the west. The highlights of its stops were the towns between Athlone (9,000 inhabitants) and the coast: Roscommon and Claremorris, with as many inhabitants as there are people living in three city apartment blocks; Castlebar, capital of County Mayo, with four thousand; and Westport with three thousand inhabitants; on one stretch, corresponding roughly to the distance between Cologne and Frankfurt, the population dwindles consistently, then comes the great water and beyond that New York with three times as many inhabitants as the whole Republic of Ireland, with more Irish than there are living in the three counties beyond Athlone.

The stations are small, the station buildings light green, the fences around them snow-white, and on the platform there usually stands a solitary boy who has taken one of his mother's trays and hung it around his neck with a leather strap: three bars of chocolate, two apples, a few rolls of peppermints, chewing gum and a comic; we wanted to entrust our last silver shilling to one of these lads, but the choice was difficult. The women were in favor of apples and peppermint; the children, of chewing gum and the comic. We compromised and bought the comic and a bar of chocolate. The comic

23

had the promising title of *Batman,* and the cover showed a man in a dark mask climbing up the outsides of houses.

The smiling boy stood there all alone on the little station in the bog. The gorse was in bloom, the fuchsia hedges were already budding; wild green hills, mounds of peat; yes, Ireland is green, very green, but its green is not only the green of meadows, it is the green of moss —certainly here, beyond Roscommon, toward County Mayo—and moss is the plant of resignation, of forsakenness. The country is forsaken, it is being slowly but steadily depopulated, and we—none of us had ever seen this strip of Ireland, or the house we had rented "somewhere in the west"—we felt a little apprehensive: in vain the women looked left and right of the train for potato fields, vegetable plots, for the fresh, unresigned green of lettuce, the darker green of peas. We divided the bar of chocolate and tried to console ourselves with *Batman,* but he was really a bad man. Not only, as the cover had promised, did he climb up the outsides of houses; one of his chief pleasures was evidently to frighten women in their sleep; he could also fly off through the air by spreading out his cloak, taking millions of dollars with him, and his deeds were described in an English such as is taught neither in Continental schools nor in the schools of England and Ireland; *Batman* was strong and terribly just, but hard, and toward the wicked he could even be cruel, for now and again he would bash in someone's teeth, a procedure fittingly rendered with the word "Screech." There was no comfort in *Batman.*

A different comfort awaited us: our red-haired conductor appeared and wrote us down with a smile for the fifth time. This mysterious process of frequent notation was now explained. We had crossed a county borderline again and were in County Mayo. Now the Irish have a strange custom: whenever the name of County Mayo is spoken (whether in praise, blame, or noncommittally), as soon as the mere word Mayo is spoken, the Irish add: "God help us!" It sounds like the response in a litany: "Lord have mercy upon us!"

The conductor disappeared with the solemn assurance that he would not have to write us down again, and we stopped at a little station. Here they unloaded what had been unloaded at all the other stations: cigarettes, that was all. We had already acquired the habit of estimating the size of the hinterland according to the size of the bales of cigarettes unloaded, and, as a look at the map proved, our calculation was correct. I walked through the train to the baggage car to see how many bales of cigarettes were still left. There was one small bale and one large one, so I knew how many more stations were ahead. The train had become alarmingly empty. I counted eighteen people, of whom we alone were six, and we seemed to have been traveling for an eternity past peat stacks, across bogs, and still there was no sign of the fresh green of lettuce, or the darker green of peas, or the bitter green of potatoes. Mayo, we said under our breath. God help us!

We stopped, the large bale of cigarettes was unloaded, and looking over the snow-white fence of the station platform were some dark faces, shaded by peaked caps, men who seemed to be guarding a column of automobiles. I had noticed these at other stations too, the cars and the waiting, watching men; it was only now that I remembered how often I had already seen them. They seemed familiar, like the bundles of cigarettes, like our conductor and the little Irish freight cars, which are scarcely more than half the size of the English and Continental ones. I entered the baggage car where our red-haired friend was squatting on the last bale of cigarettes; using the English words with care, like a novice juggler handling china plates, I asked him the significance of these dark men with the peaked caps, and what the cars were standing there for; I anticipated some kind of folkloric explanation: a modern version of an abduction, a highway robbery, but the conductor's answer was disconcertingly simple:

"Those are taxis," he said, and I breathed a sigh of relief. So whatever happens there are taxis, just as sure as there are cigarettes. The conductor seemed to have noticed my suffering: he offered me a cigarette, I accepted it gladly, he lit it for me and said with a reassuring smile:

"We'll be there in ten minutes."

Right on schedule we arrived ten minutes later in Westport. Here we were given a ceremonial reception. The stationmaster himself, a tall, dignified elderly gentleman, took up a position in front of our compartment, a friendly smile on his face, and by way of welcome raised a large engraved brass baton, symbol of his office, to his cap. He helped the ladies, helped the children, signaled for a porter, guided me deliberately but unobtrusively into his office, wrote down my name, my address in Ireland, and advised me in fatherly fashion not to depend on being able to change my money in Westport. His smile became even gentler when I showed him my German bank notes, and he said, "Nice, very nice," adding kindly:

"There's no hurry, you know, there's really no hurry, you'll pay all right. Don't worry."

Again I quoted the rate of exchange, but the dignified old man merely waved his brass baton gently from side to side, saying:

"I shouldn't worry." (And all the time the billboards were exhorting us to worry. "Think of your future. Safety first! Provide for your children!")

But I was still worrying. Our credit had brought us this far, but would it take us any farther, a two-hour stop in Westport, two and a half hours by bus to our destination, across County Mayo—God help us?

I was able to rouse the bank manager at his home; he raised his eyebrows, for it was his afternoon off. I was also able to convince him—and he lowered his eyebrows —of the relative difficulty of my position: quite a bit of money, and not a penny in my pocket! But I could not convince him of the credit standing of my bank note collection. He must have heard something about East and West German marks and of the difference in currency, and when I pointed to the word "Frankfurt" on the note he said (he must have had an A in geography): "There's a Frankfurt in the other half of Germany too"; I had no choice but to play off the Main against the Oder, which I didn't like doing, but he evidently had not had *summa cum laude* in geography, and such subtle differences, even after looking up the official rate of exchange, were too slender a foundation for a sizable credit.

"I'll have to send the money to Dublin," he said.

"The money," I said, "just the way it is?"

"Of course," he said. "What good is it to me here?"

I bowed my head: he was right, what good was it to him?

"How long will it take," I said, "for you to hear from Dublin?"

"Four days," he said.

"Four days," I said, "God help us!"

One thing at least I had learned. Could he then let me have a little credit on the basis of this bundle of bank notes? He looked thoughtfully at the bills, at "Frankfurt," at me, opened the cash drawer and gave me two pound notes.

I said nothing, signed a receipt, got one from him, and left the bank. Of course it was raining, and my family were waiting trustfully for me at the bus stop. There was hunger in their eyes, almost a yearning, the anticipation of powerful masculine, powerful paternal aid, and I made up my mind to do something which is the basis of the myth of masculinity: I made up my mind to bluff. In a grandiose gesture I invited them all to tea, to ham and eggs, salad—wherever did that come from?—to cookies and ice cream, and after paying the bill was happy to have half a crown left. That was just enough for ten cigarettes, matches, and a shilling in reserve.

I still did not know what I found out four hours later: that you can give tips on credit, and not until we had arrived, at the outer edge of County Mayo, from where there is nothing but water all the way to New York—did credit come into its full glory. The house was painted snow white, the window frames dark blue; there was a fire burning in the grate. The welcoming feast consisted of fresh salmon. The sea was pale green, up front where it rolled onto the beach, dark blue out toward the center of the bay, and a narrow, sparkling white frill was visible where the sea broke on the island.

That evening we were given something worth as much as cash—the storekeeper's account book. It was a fat book consisting of nearly eighty pages, solidly bound, with a very permanent quality about it. We had arrived, we were in Mayo—God help us?

5. Skeleton of a Human Habitation

Suddenly, on reaching the top of the hill, we saw the skeleton of the abandoned village on the slope ahead of us. No one had told us anything about it, no one had given us any warning; there are so many abandoned villages in Ireland. The church, the shortest way to the beach, had been pointed out to us, and the shop where you can buy tea, bread, butter, and cigarettes, also the newsagent's, the post office, and the little harbor where the harpooned sharks lie like capsized boats in the mud at low tide, their dark backs uppermost, unless by chance the last wave of the tide had turned up their white bellies from which the liver had been cut out—all this seemed worth mentioning, but not the abandoned village. Gray, uniform, sloping stone gables, which we saw first with no depth of perspective, like an amateurish set for a ghost film; incredulous, we tried to count them, we gave up at forty, there must have been a hundred. The next curve of the road gave us a different perspective, and now we saw them from the side: half-finished buildings that seemed to be waiting for the carpenter: gray stone walls, dark window sockets, not a stick of wood, not a shred of material, no color anywhere, like a body without hair, without eyes, without flesh and blood—the skeleton of a village, cruelly distinct in its structure. There was the main street, at the bend, by the little square, there must have been a pub. A side street, another one. Everything not made of stone gnawed away by rain, sun, and wind—and time, which patiently trickles over everything; twenty-four great drops of time a day, the acid that eats everything away as imperceptibly as resignation. . . . If anyone ever tried to paint it, this skeleton of a human habitation where a hundred years ago five hundred people may have lived: all those gray triangles and squares on the green-gray slope of the hill; if he were to include the girl with the red pullover who is just passing along the main street with a load of peat on her back, a spot of red for her pullover and a dark brown one for the peat, a lighter brown one for the girl's face, and then the white sheep huddling like lice among the ruins—he would be considered an unusually crazy painter: that's how abstract reality is. Everything not made of stone eaten away by wind, sun, rain, and time, neatly laid out along the somber slope as if for an anatomy lesson, the skeleton of a village: over there— "look, just like a spine"—the main street, a little crooked like the spine of a laborer; every little knuckle bone is there; there are the arms and the legs: the side streets and, tipped slightly to one side, the head, the church, a somewhat larger gray triangle. Left leg: the street going up the slope to the east; right leg: the other one, leading down into the valley, this one a little shortened. The skeleton of someone with a slight limp. If his skeleton were exposed in three hundred years, this is what the man might look like who is being driven by his four thin cows past us onto the meadow, leaving him the illusion that he was driving them; his right leg has been shortened by an accident, his back is crooked from the toil of cutting peat, and even his tired head will tip a little to one side when he is laid in the earth. He has already

32

overtaken us, already murmured his "nice day," before we had got our breath back sufficiently to answer him or ask him about the village.

No bombed city, no artillery-raked village ever looked like this, for bombs and shells are nothing but extended tomahawks, battle-axes, maces, with which to smash, to hack to pieces, but here there is no trace of violence; in limitless patience time and the elements have eaten away everything not made of stone, and from the earth have sprouted cushions on which these bones lie like relics, cushions of moss and grass.

No one would try to pull down a wall here or take wood (very valuable here) from an abandoned house (we call that cleaning out; no one cleans out here); and not even the children who drive the cattle home in the evening from the meadow above the deserted village, not even the children try to pull down walls or doorways; our children, when we suddenly found ourselves in the village, tried it immediately, to raze to the ground. Here no one razed anything to the ground, and the softer parts of abandoned dwellings are left to feed the wind, the rain, the sun, and time, and after sixty, seventy, or a hundred years all that is left is half-finished buildings from which no carpenter will ever again hang his wreath to celebrate the completion of a house: this, then, is what a human habitation looks like when it has been left in peace after death.

Still with a sense of awe we crossed the main street between the bare gables, entered side streets, and slowly the sense of awe lifted: grass was growing in the streets, moss had covered walls and potato plots, was creeping up the houses; and the stones of the gables, washed free

33

of mortar, were neither quarried stone nor tiles, but small boulders, just as the mountain had rolled them down its streams into the valley, door and window lintels were slabs of rock, and broad as shoulder blades were the two stone slabs sticking out of the wall where the fireplace had been: once the chain for the iron cooking pot had hung from them, pale potatoes cooking in brownish water.

We went from house to house like peddlers, and every time the short shadow on the threshold had fallen away from us the blue square of the sky covered us again; in houses where the better-off ones had once lived it was larger, where the poor had lived it was smaller: all that distinguished them now was the size of the blue square of sky. In some rooms moss was already growing, some thresholds were already covered with brownish water; here and there in the front walls you could still see the pegs for the cattle: thighbones of oxen to which the chain had been attached.

"Here's where the stove was"—"the bed over there" —"here over the fireplace hung the crucifix"—"over there a cupboard": two upright stone slabs with two vertical slabs wedged into them; here in this cupboard one of the children discovered the iron wedge, and when we drew it out it crumbled away in our hands like tinder: a hard inner piece remained about as thick as a nail which—on the children's instructions—I put in my coat pocket as a souvenir.

We spent five hours in this village, and the time passed quickly because nothing happened; we scared a few birds into flight, a sheep jumped through an empty window socket and fled up the slope at our approach; in ossified fuchsia hedges hung blood-red blossoms, in withered gorse bushes hung a yellow like dirty coins, shining quartz stuck up out of the moss like bones; no dirt in the streets, no rubbish in the streams, and not a sound to be heard. Perhaps we were waiting for the girl with the red pullover and her load of brown peat, but the girl did not come back.

On the way home when I put my hand in my pocket for the iron wedge, all my fingers found was brown dust mixed with red: the same color as the bog to the right and left of our path, and I threw it in the bog.

No one could tell us exactly when and why the village had been abandoned; there are so many deserted houses in Ireland, you can count them on any two-hour walk: that one was abandoned ten years ago, this one twenty, that one fifty or eighty years ago, and there are houses in which the nails fastening the boards to windows and doors have not yet rusted through, rain and wind cannot yet penetrate.

The old woman living in the house next to us had no idea when the village had been abandoned; when she was a little girl, around 1880, it was already deserted. Of her six children, only two have remained in Ireland: two live and work in Manchester, two in the United States, one daughter is married and living here in the village (this daughter has six children, of whom in turn two will probably go to England, two to the United States), and the oldest son has stayed home: from far off, when he comes in from the meadow with the cattle, he looks like a youth of sixteen; when he turns the corner and enters the village street you feel he must be in his mid-thirties; and when he finally passes the house and grins shyly in at the window, you see that he is fifty.

"He doesn't want to get married," said his mother, "isn't it a shame?"

Yes, it is a shame. He is so hard-working and clean; he has painted the gate red, the stone knobs on the wall red too, and the window frames under the green mossy roof bright blue; humor dwells in his eyes, and he pats his donkey affectionately.

In the evening, when we go to get the milk, we ask him about the abandoned village. But he can tell us nothing about it, nothing; he has never been there: they have no meadows over there, and their peat cuttings lie in a different direction, to the south, not far from the monument to the Irish patriot who was executed in 1799. "Have you seen it yet?" Yes, we've seen it—and Tony goes off again, a man of fifty, is transformed at the corner into a man of thirty, up there on the slope where he strokes the donkey in passing he turns into a youth of sixteen, and as he stops for a moment by the fuchsia hedge, for that moment before he disappears behind the hedge, he looks like the boy he once was.

6. Itinerant Political Dentist

"Tell me quite frankly now," said Padraic to me after the fifth glass of beer, "whether you don't think all Irishmen are half crazy?"

"No," I said, "I only think half all Irishmen are half crazy."

"You ought to have been a diplomat," said Padraic and ordered his sixth glass of beer, "but now tell me quite honestly whether you think we're a happy people."

"I think," I said, "that you are happier than you know. And if you knew how happy you are you would find a reason for being unhappy. You have many reasons for being unhappy, but you also love the poetry of unhappiness—here's to you."

We drank, and it was only after the sixth glass of beer that Padraic found the courage to ask me what he had been wanting to ask me all along.

"Tell me," he said in a low voice, "Hitler—war—I believe—not such a bad man really, only—in my opinion —he went a bit too far."

My wife looked at me encouragingly.

"Go on," she said softly in German, "don't give up, pull out the whole tooth."

"I'm no dentist," I said quietly to my wife, "and I'm tired of going to pubs in the evening. I always have to pull teeth, always the same ones. I'm sick of it."

"It's worth it," said my wife.

"Now listen, Padraic," I said amiably, "we know exactly how far Hitler went, he went over the corpses of millions of Jews, children. . . ."

A spasm of pain crossed Padraic's face. He had ordered his seventh glass of beer and said sadly: "What a pity you've let yourself be taken in by British propaganda, what a pity."

I left the beer untouched. "Come on," I said, "let me pull that tooth; it may hurt a bit, but it must be done. You won't be a really nice chap until it's done; have your teeth put right, anyway I feel like an itinerant dentist.

"Hitler was," I said, and I said everything; I had had a lot of practice, I was a good dentist already, and if the patient is a nice chap one goes about it more carefully than when one does a routine job, merely from a sense of duty. Hitler was, Hitler did, Hitler said—Pad's face twitched more and more painfully, but I had ordered whisky, I raised my glass, he swallowed, choked a little.

"Did it hurt much?" I asked cautiously.

"Yes," he said, "it hurts, and it'll go on hurting for a few days till all the pus is out."

"Don't forget to rinse your mouth, and if you're in pain come and see me, you know where I live."

"I know where you live," said Pad, "and I'll be sure to come, for I'll be sure to be in pain."

"Still," I said, "it's a good thing it's out."

Padraic was silent. "Shall we have another?" he asked sadly.

"Yes, let's," I said. "Hitler was. . . ."

"Stop," said Padraic, "please stop, the nerve's all exposed."

"Good," I said, "then it'll soon be dead, so let's have another."

"Aren't you ever sad when you have a tooth out?" asked Padraic wearily.

"For a moment, yes," I said, "but afterwards I'm glad when it doesn't fester any more."

"The stupid thing is," said Padraic, "that now I can't imagine why I like the Germans so much."

"You must like them," I said gently, "not *because of* but *in spite of* Hitler. There's nothing more embarrassing than when someone likes you for the wrong reasons. If your grandfather was a burglar, and you meet someone who likes you a lot *because* your grandfather was a burglar, that's embarrassing; other people like you because you're not a burglar, but you would like it if they thought you were nice even if you were a burglar." The eighth glass of beer arrived: Henry had ordered it, an Englishman who came here every year for his vacation.

He sat down with us and shook his head resignedly. "I don't know," he said, "why I come back to Ireland every year; I don't know how often I've told them I never liked either Pembroke or Cromwell, and that I'm not related to them, that I'm nothing but a London office worker who has a fortnight's holiday and wants to go to the seaside. I don't know why I come all this way from London every year to be told how nice I am but how terrible the English are; it's so exhausting. About Hitler . . ." said Henry.

"Please," said Padraic, "don't talk about him; I can't stand the sound of his name any more. Not now, anyway, perhaps later on. . . ."

"Good work," Henry said to me; "you seem to have done a thorough job."

"One does one's best," I said modestly, "and I've got into the habit now of pulling a certain tooth for someone every evening. I know exactly which one it is; by this time I've become quite expert in political dentistry, and I do it thoroughly and with no anesthetic."

"I'll say you do," said Padraic, "but aren't we charming people in spite of everything?"

"Of course you are," we all three said, in one voice: my wife, Henry, and I. "You're really charming," I went on, "and what's more, you're fully aware of it."

"Let's have another," said Padraic, "a nightcap!"

"And one for the road!"

"And one for the cat," I said.

"And one for the dog!"

We drank, and the clock hands still stood as they had stood for three weeks: at ten-thirty. And they would stay at ten-thirty for the next four months. Ten-thirty is closing time for country pubs during the summer, but the tourists, the visitors, liberalize hard-and-fast time. When summer comes, the landlords look for their screwdrivers, a few screws, and fix the two hands; some of them buy toy clocks with wooden hands that can be nailed down. So time stands still, and rivers of dark beer flow through the whole summer, day and night, while the police sleep the sleep of the just.

7. Portrait of an Irish Town

Limerick in the Morning

Because Limerick had given its name to the familiar little verses, I pictured it as being a cheerful place: humorous ditties, laughing girls, lots of bagpipe music, the streets resounding with merriment. We had seen a good deal of merriment on the roads between Dublin and Limerick: schoolchildren of all ages trotted gaily—many of them barefoot—through the October rain; they came out of lanes, you could see them approaching between hedges along muddy paths; children without number forming like drops into a rivulet, the rivulets forming streams, the streams little rivers—and sometimes the car drove through them as if through a river that parted readily. For a few minutes the road would remain empty, when the car had just passed through a slightly larger village, and then the drops began collecting again: Irish schoolchildren, jostling and chasing each other, often enterprisingly dressed, in variegated bits and pieces, but all of them, even those who were not merry, were at least relaxed; they often traipse for miles like that through the rain, and home again through the rain, carrying their hurling sticks, their books held together by a strap. For over a hundred miles the car drove through Irish schoolchildren, and although it was raining, and many of them were barefoot, most of them poorly dressed, almost all of them seemed cheerful.

It had seemed blasphemous when someone once said to me in Germany: The road belongs to the automobile. In Ireland I was often tempted to say: The road belongs to the cow. Indeed, cows are sent as freely to pasture as children to school: they fill the road with their herds, turn round haughtily when you blow your horn, and the driver has a chance here to show a sense of humor, behave calmly, and test his skill. He drives carefully right up to the herd, timidly forces his way into the condescendingly formed passage and, the minute he has reached the leading cow and overtaken it, he can step on the gas and count himself lucky to have escaped a danger—and what is more exciting, what better stimulus is there for human gratitude, than danger averted? So the Irish driver remains a creature to whom gratitude is not foreign; he must constantly fight for his life, his rights, and his speed: against schoolchildren and cows. He would never be able to coin a snobbish slogan such as: The road belongs to the automobile. Ireland is a long way from deciding who the road belongs to. And how beautiful these roads are: walls, walls, trees, walls and hedges; the stones of Irish walls would be enough to build the tower of Babel, but Irish ruins are proof that it would be useless to begin such a building. In any event, these beautiful roads do not belong to the automobile; they belong to whoever happens to occupy them and whoever allows those desiring passage to prove their skill. Some roads belong to the donkey: donkeys playing truant from school, there are plenty of those in Ireland; they nibble away at the hedges, mournfully contemplate the countryside—turning their rumps toward the passing car. Whatever else, the road does not belong to the automobile.

Much contentment, much merriment among the cows, the donkeys, and the schoolchildren, came our way between Dublin and Limerick, and who, thinking of Limericks, could approach Limerick without picturing a cheerful town? Where the roads had been dominated by cheerful schoolchildren, complacent cows, pensive donkeys, now suddenly they were empty. The children seemed to have reached school, the cows their pasture, and the donkeys seemed to have been called to order. Dark clouds came up from the Atlantic—and the streets of Limerick were dark and empty. Only the milk bottles in the doorways were white, almost too white, and the seagulls splintering the gray of the sky, clouds of white plump gulls, splinters of white that for a second or two joined to form a great patch of white. Moss shimmered green on ancient walls from the eighth, ninth, and all subsequent centuries, and the walls of the twentieth century were hardly distinguishable from those of the eighth —they too were moss-covered, they too were ruined. In butcher shops gleamed whitish-red sides of beef, and the preschool children of Limerick showed their originality here: hanging on to pigs' trotters, to oxtails, they swung to and fro between the hunks of meat: grinning pale faces. Irish children are very inventive; but are these the only inhabitants of this town?

We parked the car near the cathedral and strolled slowly through the dismal street. The gray Shannon rushed along under old bridges: this river was too big, too wide, too wild for this gloomy little town. Loneliness seized us, we felt sad, deserted between moss, old walls, and the many painfully white milk bottles that seemed destined for people long dead; even the children swinging from the sides of beef in the unlit butcher shops seemed like ghosts. There is a way of fighting the loneliness that can seize one suddenly in a strange town: buy something; a picture postcard, or some chewing gum, a pencil or cigarettes: hold something in your hand, participate in the life of this town by buying something—but would there be anything to buy here in Limerick, on a Thursday at half-past ten in the morning? Would we not wake up all of a sudden to find ourselves standing in the rain beside the car somewhere on the highway, and Limerick would have disappeared like a mirage, a mirage of the rain? So painfully white were the milk bottles—not quite so white the screaming gulls.

The old part of Limerick stands in relation to the new part like the Ile de la Cité to the rest of Paris, with the proportion of old Limerick to the Ile de la Cité being about one to three and that of the new Limerick to Paris one to two hundred. Danes, Normans, much later the Irish, occupied this lovely somber island in the Shannon; gray bridges link it to the banks, the gray Shannon rushes by, and up there, where the bridge joins the land, a monument has been erected to a stone—or a stone has been placed on a pedestal. At this stone the Irish were promised freedom of religious expression and a treaty was concluded that was later revoked by the English parliament, so Limerick is also sometimes called "the town of the broken treaty."

In Dublin we had been told: "Limerick is the most devout city in the world." So we would only have had to look at the calendar to know why the streets were so deserted, the milk bottles unopened, the shops empty: Limerick was at church, at eleven o'clock on a Thursday morning. Suddenly, before we had reached the center of modern Limerick, the church doors opened, the streets filled up, the milk bottles were removed from the doorways. It was like an invasion: the inhabitants of Limerick were occupying their town. Even the post office was opened, and the bank opened its wickets. Everything looked disconcertingly normal, close, and human, where five minutes ago we seemed to be walking through an abandoned medieval town.

We bought a number of things to reassure ourselves of the existence of this town: cigarettes, soap, picture postcards, and a jigsaw puzzle. We smoked the cigarettes, sniffed the soap, wrote on the postcards, packed up the jigsaw puzzle, and went cheerfully off to the post office. Here there was a slight hitch—the postmistress had not yet returned from church, and her subordinate was unable to clarify what had to be clarified: how much did it cost to send printed matter (the jigsaw puzzle) weighing eight ounces to Germany? The young lady looked imploringly at the picture of the Madonna, with the candle flickering in front of it; but Mary was silent, she only smiled, as she has been smiling for four hundred years, and the smile said: patience. Strange weights were brought out, a strange scale, bright green Customs forms were spread out in front of us, tariff books open and closed, but there remained only one solution: patience. We practiced it. After all, who would want to send a jigsaw puzzle as printed matter from Limerick to Germany in October? Who does not know that the Feast of the Rosary, although not a whole holiday, is more than a half-holiday?

Later on, though, long after the jigsaw puzzle lay in the letter box, we saw the scepticism flowering in hard, sad eyes: melancholy shining in blue eyes, in the eyes of the gypsy selling pictures of saints on the street, and in the eyes of the hotel manageress, in the eyes of the taxi driver—thorns around the rose, arrows in the heart of the most devout city in the world.

Limerick in the Evening

Ravished, robbed of their seals, the milk bottles stood gray, empty, and dirty in doorways and on window sills, waiting sadly for the morning when they would be replaced by their fresh, radiant sisters, and the gulls were not white enough to replace the angelic radiance of the innocent milk bottles; the gulls bobbed along on the Shannon, which, pressed between walls, increases its speed for two hundred yards. Sour, gray-green seaweed covered the walls; it was low tide, and it almost looked as if Old Limerick were exposing itself indecently, lifting its dress, showing parts that are otherwise covered by water; rubbish was waiting to be washed away by the tide; dim lights burned in the bookies' offices, drunks staggered through the gutters, and the children who that morning had swung from sides of beef in butcher shops now showed that there is a level of poverty for which even the safety pin is too expensive: string is cheaper, and it works just as well. What eight years ago had been a cheap jacket, but new, now served as jacket, overcoat, trousers, and shirt in one; the grown-up sleeves rolled up, string around the middle; and held in the hand—innocently shining like milk, that manna that is to be found, always fresh and cheap, in the last hamlet in Ireland—ice cream. Marbles roll across the sidewalk; now and again a glance at the bookies' office where Father is just putting part of his unemployment pay on Crimson Cloud. Deeper and deeper sinks the comforting darkness, while the marbles click against the worn steps leading up to the bookie's office. Is Father going on to the next bookie, to put something on Gray Moth, to the third, to put something on Innisfree? There is no dearth of bookies here in Old Limerick. The marbles roll against the step, snow-white drops of ice cream fall into the gutter where they remain for a second like stars on the mud, only a second, before their innocence melts away into the mud.

No, Father is not going to another bookie, he is just going to the pub; the marbles can also be clicked against the worn steps of the pub: will Father give them some more money for ice cream? He does. One for Johnny too, and for Paddy, for Sheila and Moira, for Mother and Auntie, perhaps for Granny too? Of course, as long as there's any money left. Isn't Crimson Cloud going to win? Of course she is. She *has* to win, damn it; if she doesn't win, then—"Look out, John, don't bang down your glass so hard on the counter. How about another?" Yes. Crimson Cloud *has* to win.

And when there's no more string, the fingers will do, thin, dirty, numb children's fingers of the left hand, while the right hand shoves marbles, throws them or rolls them. "Come on Ned, give us a lick," and suddenly in the evening darkness the clear sound of a girl's voice.

"There's a service this evening, aren't you going?"

Grins, hesitation, head-shaking.

"Yes, we're coming."

"Not me."

"Oh come on."

"No."

"Oh well—"

"No."

Marbles click against the worn steps of the pub.

My companion was trembling; he was a victim of the most bitter and stupid prejudice of all: that people who are badly dressed are dangerous—more dangerous anyway than the well-dressed ones. He ought to tremble in the bar of the Shelbourne Hotel in Dublin at least as much as here, behind King John's Castle in Limerick. If only they were more dangerous, these ragged ones, if only they were as dangerous as those in the bar of the Shelbourne Hotel who don't look dangerous at all. At this moment a woman, the owner of an eating place, comes rushing out after a boy who has bought sixpenn'orth of potato chips and in her opinion has poured too much vinegar on them from the bottle he took from the table.

"You wretch, d'you want to ruin me?"

Will he throw the chips in her face? No—he can't think of anything to say, only his panting child's breast answers: long-drawn-out whistling sounds come from the weak organ of his lungs. Did not Swift, more than two hundred years ago, in 1729, write his bitterest satire, the "Modest Proposal for Preventing the Children of Poor People from Being a Burden to Their Parents or

48

the Country" by suggesting to the government that the estimated number of 120,000 babies born annually be offered to the wealthy English *as food?*—precise, gruesome description of a project that was to serve a number of purposes, among others a reduction in the number of Papists.

The battle over the six drops of vinegar is still not over, the woman's hand is raised threateningly, long whistling sounds come from the boy's chest. Indifferent people shuffle by, drunks stagger, children carrying prayer books run so as to be in time for the evening service. But the savior was approaching: tall, fat, bloated, his nose must have been bleeding, there were dark patches on his face around mouth and nose; he had also advanced from safety pin to string: there had not been enough for his shoes, they were gaping. He went up to the woman, bowed to her, pretended to kiss her hand, drew a ten-shilling note from his pocket, presented it to her—startled, she accepted it—and said courteously:

"May I request you, Madam, to regard these ten shillings as sufficient payment for the six drops of vinegar?"

Silence in the darkness behind King John's Castle, then the man with the blood-stained face suddenly went on in a low voice:

"May I moreover remind you that it is time for the evening service? Please convey my respectful regards to the priest."

He staggered on, the boy ran off scared, and the woman was alone. Suddenly tears were streaming down her face, and she ran weeping into the house, her sobs still audible when the door had closed behind her.

The sea had not yet allowed the kindly water to rise, the walls were still naked and dirty, and the gulls not white enough. King John's Castle reared grimly out of the darkness, a tourist attraction hemmed in by tenements from the twenties, and the tenements of the twentieth century looked more dilapidated than King John's Castle of the thirteenth; the dim light from weak bulbs could not compete with the massive shadow of the castle, everything was submerged in sour darkness.

Ten shillings for six drops of vinegar! The man who lives poetry instead of writing it pays ten thousand per cent interest. Where was he, the dark, blood-stained drunk, who had had enough string for his jacket but not for his shoes? Had he plunged into the Shannon, into the gurgling gray narrows between the two bridges which the gulls used as a free toboggan? They were still circling in the darkness, they alighted on the gray waters, between one bridge and the other, flew up to repeat the game; endless; insatiable.

Singing came flooding out of churches, voices of chanting priests, taxis brought travelers from Shannon airport, green buses swayed through the gray darkness, black, bitter beer flowed behind curtained pub windows. Crimson Cloud *has* to win.

The great Sacred Heart shone crimson in the church where the evening service was already over; candles were burning, stragglers were praying, incense and candle warmth, silence, in which only the shuffling footsteps of the sacristan were to be heard as he straightened the curtains of the confessionals, emptied the offering boxes. The Sacred Heart shone crimson.

How much is the fare for these fifty, sixty, seventy years from the dock that is called birth to the spot in the ocean where the shipwreck occurs?

Clean parks, clean monuments, black, severe, well-behaved streets: somewhere near here Lola Montez was born. Ruins from the time of the Rebellion, boarded-up houses that are not yet ruins, the sound of rats moving around behind the black boards, warehouses cracked open and left to the disintegration of time, green-gray slime on exposed walls, and the black beer flows to the health of Crimson Cloud, who is not going to win. Streets, streets, flooded for a few moments by those coming from evening service, streets in which the houses seem to get smaller and smaller; prison walls, convent walls, church walls, barrack walls; a lieutenant coming off duty props his bicycle by the door of his tiny house and stumbles over his children on the threshold.

Incense again, candle warmth, silence, people at prayer who cannot bear to part from the crimson Sacred Heart being gently reminded by the sacristan please to go home. Head-shaking. "But—," whispered arguments on the part of the sacristan. Head-shaking. Firmly glued to the kneeling bench. Who is going to count the prayers, the curses, and who has the Geiger counter that could register the hopes concentrated this evening on Crimson Cloud? Four slim fetlocks, there is a mortgage on these that nobody is going to be able to redeem. And when Crimson Cloud does not win, the grief must be quenched with as much dark beer as was needed to nourish the hope. Marbles are still clicking against the worn steps of the pub, against the worn steps of churches and bookies' offices.

It was much later that I discovered the last innocent milk bottle, as virginal as it had been in the morning; it was standing in the doorway of a tiny house whose shutters were closed. In the next doorway an elderly woman, gray-haired, slatternly, only the cigarette in her face was white. I stopped.

"Where is he?" I asked softly.

"Who?"

"The one the milk belongs to. Is he still asleep?"

"No," she said quietly, "he emigrated today."

"And left the milk?"

"Yes."

"And the light on?"

"Is it still on?"

"Can't you see?"

I leaned forward, close to the yellow chink in the door, and looked in, where in a tiny hall a towel was still hanging on a doorknob and a hat on the peg, where a dirty plate with the remains of some potatoes lay on the floor.

"So he has, he's left the light on, but what's the difference: they won't be sending him the bill to Australia."

"To Australia?"

"Yes."

"And the milk bill?"

"Hasn't paid that either."

The white of the cigarette was already dwindling toward her dark lips, and she shuffled back to her doorway. "Oh well," she said, "he could have turned out the light."

Limerick slept, under a thousand rosaries, under curses, floated on dark beer; watched over by a single snow-white milk bottle, it was dreaming of Crimson Cloud and the crimson Sacred Heart.

8. When God Made Time . . .

That a church service can only begin when the priest
arrives is obvious; but that a movie can only begin when
all the priests, the local ones as well as those on vacation,
are assembled in full strength is somewhat surprising to
the foreigner used to Continental customs. He can only
hope that the priest and his friends will soon finish their
supper and their postprandial chat; that they do not
overindulge in reminiscences: the range of do-you-
remember conversations is inexhaustible; that Latin
teacher, that math teacher, not to mention that history
teacher!

The movie is supposed to start at 9 P.M., but if there is
one thing subject to change it is this hour. Even the
vaguest formula for an appointment, as when one says
"around nine," is by comparison a term of utmost preci-
sion, for "around nine" is over by half-past nine, when
"around ten" begins; this "9 P.M.," the unadorned preci-
sion with which it appears on the poster, is a snare and a
delusion.

The strange thing is that no one is in the least annoyed
at the delay. "When God made time," the Irish say, "He
made plenty of it." There is no doubt that this saying is
as much to the point as it is worth meditating on: if we
imagine time to be a substance that has been given to us
in order that we may settle our affairs here on earth, we
have certainly been given enough, for there is always

"plenty of time." The man who has no time is a monster, a fiend: he steals time from somewhere, secretes it. (How much time must have been wasted, how much must have been stolen, to make the unjustly famed military punctuality so proverbial: billions of stolen hours of time are the price for this prodigal kind of punctuality, not to mention the monsters of our day who have no time! They always seem to me like people with not enough skin. . . .)

There is ample time to meditate, for by now it is long after nine-thirty, perhaps the priests have got as far as the biology teacher, a minor subject after all, possibly a spur to hope. But even those who do not make use of the delay for meditation are looked after: records are played unstintingly, chocolate, ice cream, cigarettes are offered for sale, for here—what a blessing—smoking is permitted. There would probably be a rebellion if smoking at the movies were prohibited, for among the Irish the passion for moviegoing is coupled with that of smoking.

The rosy glow from the shells on the walls gives out a feeble light, and in the semidarkness the atmosphere is as lively as at a fair. Conversations are carried on across four rows of seats, jokes are shouted over eight; up front in the cheap seats the children are making the kind of cheerful racket heard otherwise only in school breaks; chocolates are proffered, cigarette brands exchanged, somewhere out of the dark comes the promising squeak of a cork being pulled out of a whisky bottle; make-up is renewed, perfume sprayed; somebody starts singing, and for those who do not allow that all these human sounds, movements, and activities are worth the trouble of occupying the passing time, there remains time for meditation; when God made time, He made plenty of it. Certainly in the use of time there is as much extravagance as thrift, and paradoxically enough it is the time-squanderers who also manage to save it, for they always have time when you ask them for some; time to take someone quickly to the station or the hospital; just as you can always ask money-squanderers for money, so time-squanderers are the savings banks where God deposits His time, keeping a reserve for when some is suddenly needed on an occasion where one of those people who never have enough time has spent it in the wrong place.

However: we have gone to the movies to see Ann Blyth, not to meditate, although meditation comes surprisingly easily and is pleasant enough in this fairground of lighthearted gaiety, where bog farmers, peat cutters, and fishermen offer cigarettes to and accept chocolates from seductively smiling ladies who drive around during the day in great cars, where the retired colonel chats with the postman about the merits and demerits of East Indians. Here classless society has become reality. It is a pity, though, that the air gets so stale: perfume, lipstick, cigarettes, the bitter smell of peat from clothes, even the music from the phonograph records seems to smell: it exudes the raw eroticism of the thirties, and the seats, splendidly upholstered in red velvet—if you are lucky you get one where the springs are not yet broken—these seats, probably deemed elegant in 1880 in Dublin (they must have seen Sullivan's operas, perhaps also Yeats, Synge, and O'Casey, and early Shaw), these seats smell the way old velvet smells that resists the harshness of the vacuum cleaner, the savagery of the brush—and the theater is an unfinished new building, still without proper ventilation.

Well, the chatting priests and chaplains don't seem to have got to the biology teacher after all, or are they discussing the janitor (an inexhaustible topic), or their first furtive cigarettes? Those who find the air too stale can go out and lean for a few minutes against the wall of the building: a clear, mild evening outside; the light from the lighthouse on Clare Island, twelve miles away, is not yet visible; the eye falls on the quiet sea across thirty, forty miles, beyond the edge of the bay as far as the mountains of Connemara and Galway—and looking to the right, westward, you see high cliffs, the last two miles of Europe lying between you and America. Wild, the perfect setting for a witches' sabbath, covered with bog and heather, rises the most westerly of Europe's mountains, a sheer drop of two thousand feet on the ocean side; facing you on its slope in the dark green of the bog, a paler, cultivated square patch with a large gray house: this is where Captain Boycott lived, the man for whom the inhabitants invented boycotting: this is where the world was given a new word; a few hundred yards above this house, the remains of a crashed airplane —American pilots, a fraction of a second too early, had thought they had reached the open sea, the smooth surface between them and their native land: Europe's last cliff, the last jag of that continent, was their doom.

Azure spreads over the sea, in varying layers, varying shades; wrapped in this azure are green islands, looking like great patches of bog, black ones, jagged, rearing up out of the ocean like stumps of teeth. . . .

Finally (or unfortunately—I am not sure which) the priests have finished or broken off their school reminiscences, they have also arrived to look at the feast promised by the poster: Ann Blyth. The rosy shells are dimmed, the racket in the cheap seats dies away, this whole classless society sinks into silent anticipation, while, honeyed, colored, and wide-screened, the film begins. Now and again one of the four- or three-year-old children begins to bawl when pistols bang too realistically, or blood, looking too genuine, flows from the hero's forehead, or dark-red drops even appear on the heroine's neck: Oh, must this lovely neck be pierced? It isn't permanently pierced, don't worry; a piece of chocolate quickly stuffed into the mouth of the bawling child, and pain and chocolate melt away in the darkness. At the end of the film one has that feeling unknown since childhood—of having eaten too much chocolate, indulged in too many sweets: Oh that painful precious heartburn from intensely enjoyed forbidden pleasures! After so much saccharine a spicy preview: black and white, gambling hell—hard thin women, ugly bold heroes, more of the inevitable pistol shots, more chocolate stuffed into the mouth of the three-year-old. A program of generous dimensions; it lasts three hours, and here too, when the rosy shells begin to glow again, the doors are opened, on people's faces what is always to be seen on people's faces at the end of a movie: a slight embarrassment, disguised by a smile; one is a little ashamed of the emotion one has involuntarily invested. The beautiful creature from the fashion magazine climbs into her great car, enormous blood-red tail lights, glowing like lumps of peat, move away toward the hotel—the peat

57

cutter plods wearily off to his cottage; silent grown-ups, while the children, twittering, laughing, scattering far into the night, repeat to each other the story of the film.

It is past midnight, the light from Clare Island lighthouse has been shining across for some time, the blue silhouettes of the mountains are deep black, a few yellow lights far off in the bog; Grandma is waiting there, or Mother, or the husband or wife, to be told what they are going to see for themselves in a day or two, and they will sit by the fire till two, three in the morning, for—when God made time, He made plenty of it.

Donkeys bray in the warm summer night, passing on their abstract song, that crazy noise as of badly oiled door hinges, rusty pumps—incomprehensible signals, magnificent and too abstract to sound credible, an expression of limitless pain and yet resignation. Cyclists whir by like bats on unlit wire steeds, until finally only the quiet peaceful footsteps of the pedestrians fill the night.

9. Thoughts on Irish Rain

The rain here is absolute, magnificent, and frightening. To call this rain bad weather is as inappropriate as to call scorching sunshine fine weather.

You can call this rain bad weather, but it is not. It is simply weather, and weather means rough weather. It reminds us forcibly that its element is water, falling water. And water is hard. During the war I once watched a burning aircraft going down on the Atlantic coast; the pilot landed it on the beach and fled from the exploding machine. Later I asked him why he hadn't landed the burning plane on the water, and he replied: "Because water is harder than sand."

I never believed him, but now I understood: water is hard.

And how much water can collect over three thousand miles of ocean, water that rejoices in at last reaching people, houses, terra firma, after having fallen only into water, only into itself. How can rain enjoy always falling into water?

When the electric light goes out, when the first tongue of a puddle licks its way under the door, silent and smooth, gleaming in the firelight; when the toys which the children have left lying around, when corks and bits of wood suddenly start floating and are borne forward by the tongue, when the children come downstairs, scared, and huddle in front of the fire (more surprised than scared, for they also sense the joy in this meeting of wind and rain and that this howling is a howl of delight), then we know we would not have been as worthy of the ark as Noah was. . . .

Inlander's madness, to open the door to see what's up outside. Everything's up: the roof tiles, the roof gutters, even the house walls, do not inspire much confidence (for here they build temporarily, although, if they don't emigrate, they live forever in these temporary quarters —while in Europe they build for eternity without knowing whether the next generation will benefit from so much solidity).

It is a good thing always to have candles, the Bible, and a little whisky in the house, like sailors prepared for a storm; also a pack of cards, some tobacco, knitting needles and wool for the women; for the storm has a lot of breath, the rain holds a lot of water, and the night is long. Then when a second tongue of rain advances from the window and joins the first one, when the toys float slowly along the narrow tongue toward the window, it is a good thing to look up in the Bible whether the promise to send no more floods has really been given. It has been given: we can light the next candle, the next cigarette, shuffle the cards again, pour some more whisky, abandon ourselves to the drumming of the rain, the howling of the wind, the click of the knitting needles. The promise has been given.

It was some time before we heard the knocking on the door—at first we had taken it for the banging of a loose bolt, then for the rattle of the storm, then we realized it was human hands, and the naïveté of the Continental mentality can be measured from the fact that I expressed the opinion it might be the man from the electric company. Almost as naïve as expecting the bailiff to appear on the high seas.

Quickly the door was opened, a dripping figure of a man pulled in, the door shut, and there he stood; with his cardboard suitcase sopping wet, water running out of his sleeves, his shoes, from his hat, it almost seemed as if water were running out of his eyes—this is how swimmers look after taking part in a lifesaving contest fully clothed; but such ambitions were foreign to this man: he had merely come from the bus stop, fifty paces through this rain, had mistaken our house for his hotel, and was by occupation a clerk in a law office in Dublin.

"D'you mean to say the bus is running in this weather?"

"Yes," he said, "it is, and only a bit behind schedule. But it was more of a swim than a drive . . . and you're sure this isn't a hotel?"

"Yes, but. . . ."

He—Dermot was his name—turned out, when he was dry, to know his Bible, to be a good card-player, a good storyteller, a good whisky-drinker; moreover, he showed us how to bring water quickly to the boil on a tripod in the fireplace, how to broil lamb chops on the same ancient tripod, how to toast bread on long forks, the purpose of which we had not yet discovered—and it was not till the small hours that he confessed to knowing a little German; he had been a prisoner-of-war in Germany, and he told our children something they will never forget, must never forget: how he buried the little gypsy children who had died during the evacuation of the Stuthof concentration camp; they were so small—he

61

showed us—and he had dug graves in the frozen ground to bury them.

"But why did they have to die?" asked one of the children.

"Because they were gypsies."

"But that's no reason—you don't have to die because of that."

"No," said Dermot, "that's no reason, you don't have to die because of that."

We stood up; it was light now, and at that moment it became quiet outside. Wind and rain had gone away, the sun came up over the horizon, and a great rainbow arched over the sea; it was so close we thought we could see it in substance—as thin as soap bubbles was the skin of the rainbow.

Corks and bits of wood were still bobbing about in the puddle when we went upstairs to the bedrooms.

10. The Most Beautiful Feet in the World

To take her mind off her worries, the doctor's young wife had begun to knit, but she soon threw the needles and ball of wool into the corner of the sofa; then she opened a book, read a few lines, shut the book again; she poured herself some whisky, pensively emptied the glass in small sips, opened another book, closed that one again too; she sighed, reached for the telephone receiver, replaced it: who was there to call?

One of her children muttered in its sleep, the young woman walked softly across the passage into the children's bedroom, covered the children up again, smoothed sheets and blankets on four children's beds. In the passage she stopped in front of the large map which, yellow with age, covered with mysterious signs, looks almost like an enlargement of the map of Treasure Island; surrounded by sea, the mountains dark brown like mahogany, the valleys light brown, the roads and paths black, the little cultivated patches around the tiny villages green, and everywhere the blue tongue of the sea thrusting into the island in bays: small crosses: churches, chapels, cemeteries; little harbors, lighthouses, cliffs—slowly the woman's forefinger with the silver-lacquered nail moves along the road by which her husband left two hours ago: a village, two miles of bog, a village, three miles of bog, a church—the young woman crosses herself as if she were really driving past the church—five

63

miles of bog, a village, two miles of bog, a church—a sign of the cross; the filling station, Teddy O'Malley's bar, Beckett's shop, three miles of bog—slowly the silvery fingernail moves across the map like a shiny toy car, until it reaches the Sound where the thick black line of the highway swings across the bridge to the mainland, while the road her husband has to take, now only a fine black line, follows the edge of the island and in places coincides with the edge. The map is dark brown here, the coastline jagged and uneven like the cardiogram of an irregular heartbeat, and someone has written with a ballpoint on the blue of the sea: 200 feet—380 feet—300 feet, and next to each of these figures is an arrow to show that the figures apply not to the depth of the sea but to the height of the cliffs, which at these places coincide with the road. Time and again the silvery fingernail halts, for the young woman knows every step of the way; she has often accompanied her husband on his calls at the only house along that six-mile stretch of coast. On sunny days tourists enjoy this drive, with a slight shiver at being able for several miles to look down perpendicularly from the car onto the writhing white sea; a moment's inattention, and the car will be wrecked down there on those cliffs where many a ship has foundered. The road is wet, strewn with stones and rocks, covered with sheep dung at the places where the old sheep trails cross the road—suddenly the fingernail halts: here the road descends steeply into a little bay, rises again on the other side: the sea roars into a canyonlike gorge; it is millions of years old, this rage that has eaten deep in under the rocks—again the finger halts: here there used to be a little cemetery for unbaptized children; a single grave is

64

still to be seen, bordered with pieces of quartz: all the other bones have been carried away by the sea—the car now carefully crosses an old bridge that has lost its railing, it turns, and the glare of the headlights reveals the waving arms of waiting women: in this remote corner lives Aedan McNamara, whose wife is expecting a child tonight.

The doctor's young wife shivers, shakes her head, walks slowly back to the living room, piles on more peat, pokes the glowing embers till the flames leap up; the woman reaches for her knitting bundle, throws it back into the corner of the sofa, gets up, goes over to the mirror, stands there for half a minute in thought, head lowered, suddenly throws back her head and looks into her face: with the heavy make-up her child's face looks even more childlike, almost like a doll's, but this doll has four children. Dublin is so far away—Grafton Street—O'Connell Bridge—the wharves; movies and dances—the Abbey Theatre—every weekday morning at eleven, Mass at St. Theresa's, where you have to arrive early to find a seat—with a sigh the young woman goes back to the fireplace. Must Aedan McNamara's wife always have her children at night and always in September? But Aedan McNamara works from March to December in England, comes home only at Christmas, for three months, to cut his peat, repaint the house, repair the roof, do a bit of furtive fishing along this rugged stretch of coast, to look for jetsam—and to beget the next child: so Aedan McNamara's children always come in September, around the twenty-third: nine months after Christmas, when the great storms come, and the angry foam makes the sea snow-white for miles. Aedan is probably now standing at a bar in Birmingham, anxious like all expectant fathers, cursing the obstinacy of his wife, who refuses to budge from this solitude: a dark-haired, defiant beauty, whose children are all September children; among the dilapidated houses in the village, she lives in the only one that has not yet been abandoned. At this spot on the coast, whose beauty hurts because on sunny days you can see for twenty, thirty miles without a human habitation: only azure, islands that are not real, and the sea. Behind the house rises the bare hillside, four hundred feet high, and three hundred paces from the house the coast falls a sheer three hundred feet; black, naked rocks, gorges, caves penetrating fifty, seventy yards into the rocks; from which on stormy days the foam rises up threateningly, like a white finger, the storm carrying the joints away one by one.

From here, Nuala McNamara went to New York to sell nylons at Woolworth's, John became a teacher in Dublin, Tommy a Jesuit in Rome, Brigid married and went to live in London—but Mary clung doggedly to this hopeless, lonely spot, where every September for four years she has borne a child.

"Come on the twenty-fourth, Doctor, around eleven, and I guarantee you'll not come in vain."

In ten days she will be walking with her father's old knobbed stick along the edge of the steep cliffs, watching out for her sheep and for those articles which for coast-dwellers are a substitute for the sweepstake (in which of course they also have a ticket), with the sharp eye of the coast-dweller she will be looking for jetsam, reaching for the binoculars when her predatory eye detects from the outline and color of an object that it is not a rock. Does she not know every boulder, every chunk of rock, along these six miles of coast—does she not know every cliff at every tide? In October alone of last year, after the great storms, she found three bales of crude rubber; she hid them in the cave above the high-water line where centuries ago her ancestors hid teak-wood, copper, brandy kegs, whole ship's equipment, from the eyes of the coast guards.

The young woman with the silvery nails smiles, she has had her second whisky, a large one, which finally allayed her anxiety; you just have to stop and think after every sip: this firewater affects you not only in depth but also in breadth. Has she not herself borne four children, and has not her husband already returned three times from this drive through the September night?

The young woman goes back into the passage, listens through the open door once again to the quiet breathing of her children, smiles, places her silvery fingernail once more on the old map, moves it forward while she calculates: half an hour along the slippery road to the Sound, three-quarters of an hour to Aedan McNamara's house, and if the child really does come punctually, if the two women from the next village are already there—perhaps two hours for the birth; another half hour for the cup of tea, which can be anything from a cup of tea to a hearty meal; another three-quarters of an hour and another half hour for the drive back: five hours altogether. John left at nine, so around two she ought to be able to see the headlights of his car where the road comes up over the hill. The young woman looks at her watch: just past

67

twelve-thirty. Once more slowly with the silver finger across the map: bog, village, church, bog, village, a barracks that has been blown up, bog, village, bog.

The young woman returns to the fire, puts on fresh peat, pokes it, stands thinking, reaches for the newspaper. On the front page are the personal announcements: births, deaths, engagements, and a special column called "In Memoriam": "In memory of dearly beloved Moira McDermott, who died one year ago in Tipperary. Kindly Jesus, have mercy on her soul. May you who think of her this day address a prayer to Jesus." Two columns, forty times, the young woman with the silvery nails prays "Kindly Jesus, have mercy on him—have mercy on her" for the Joyces and McCarthys, the Molloys and Gallaghers.

Then come the silver weddings, the rings lost, the purses found, official announcements.

Seven nuns going to Australia, six going to North America, smiled at the press photographer. Twenty-seven newly ordained priests smiled at the press photographer. Fifteen bishops advising on the problems of emigration did likewise.

On page 3 the stud bull who carries on a line of prize-winning pedigree bulls; then come Malenkov, Bulganin, and Serov—turn to the next page; a prize-winning sheep, a garland of flowers between his horns; a girl who won first prize in a singing contest showed the press photographer her pretty face and her ugly teeth. Thirty graduates of a boarding school met again after fifteen years: some of them have put on weight, others stand out tall and slim from the group, even in the newspaper picture their make-up is clearly visible: mouths like India ink, eyebrows like delicate forceful brush strokes. The thirty women were assembled at Mass, at tea, at the evening rosary.

The three daily comics: Rip Kirby, Hopalong Cassidy, and The Heart of Juliet Jones. Juliet Jones' heart is hard.

Casually, while her eyes were already half-occupied with the movie advertisement, the young woman reads an account of West Germany, "How They Make Use of Their Religious Freedom in West Germany." For the first time in the history of that country—the young woman reads—there is complete freedom of religious observance in West Germany. Poor Germany, the young woman thinks, and adds a "Kindly Jesus, have mercy on them."

She has long since glanced at the movie advertisement, now her eyes dwell greedily on the column entitled "Wedding Bells": a long column; so Dermot O'Hara has married Siobhan O'Shaughnessy: occupation and residence of both sets of parents, of the best man, the bridesmaids, and the witnesses are given in detail.

With a sigh, secretly hoping that an hour has gone by, the young woman looks at her watch; but it is only half an hour, and she lowers her face again toward the newspaper. Tours are advertised: to Rome, Lourdes, Lisieux, to the Rue du Barc in Paris, to the grave of Katharina Labouré; and there for a few shillings you can have your name inscribed in the *Golden Book of Prayer*. A new mission house has been opened: the founders face the camera with beaming smiles. In a tiny place in County Mayo, four hundred and fifty inhabitants, there has been a real festival thanks to the activities of the local festival committee: there were donkey races and sack races, a broad-jump contest and a slow-bicycle race: the boy who won the slow-bicycle race grinned as he faced the press photographer: a frail apprentice in the grocery business was the cleverest at using the brakes.

A storm has arisen outside, you can hear the roar of the surf, and the young woman puts aside the paper, gets up, goes to the window, and looks out into the bay: the rocks are as black as ancient ink, although the coin of the moon floats clear and full above the bay; this clear, cold light does not penetrate the sea: it merely clings to its surface, as water clings to glass, gives the beach a soft rust color, lies on the bog like mildew; the little light down in the harbor wavers, the black boats sway. . . .

There's certainly no harm in saying a few "Kindly Jesus, have mercy on her" for Mary McNamara too; now there are beads of sweat on the pale, proud face that in some inexplicable way expresses both hardness and goodness: a shepherd's face, a fisherman's face, perhaps Joan of Arc looked like that. . . .

The young woman turns away from the coldness of the moon, smokes a cigarette, decides against a third whisky, picks up the paper again, runs her eye casually over it while her mind is busy saying "Kindly Jesus, have mercy on her"—while she glances at the sports page, the market report, shipping movements—she is thinking of Mary McNamara: now water has been heated up in the magnificent copper cauldron over the peat fire; in that red-gold pot as big as a child's bathtub which one of Mary's ancestors is said to have salvaged from a wreck of the Spanish Armada: perhaps Spanish sailors brewed beer, cooked their soup, in it. Oil

lamps and candles are burning now in front of all the
saints' pictures, and Mary's feet, looking for support,
press against the bars of the bed, slip, and now you can
see her feet: white, delicate, strong, the most beautiful
feet the doctor's young wife has ever seen—and she has
seen many feet: in the orthopedic clinic in Dublin, in one
of those places for people with foot ailments where she
used to take a job during vacation: the poor ugly feet of
those who no longer use their feet; and the young
woman had seen naked feet on many beaches: in Dublin,
in Kiliney, Rossbeigh, Sandymount, Malahide, Bray, and
in the summer here when the vacationers come—never
has she seen such beautiful feet as those of Mary McNamara. One ought to be able to compose ballads, she
thinks with a sigh, to praise Mary's feet: feet that climb
over rocks, over cliffs, wade through bog, walk for miles
along the road—feet that are straining now against the
bars of the bed, to press the child out of her body. Feet
such as I have never seen even on a film star, surely the
most beautiful feet in the world: white, delicate, strong,
almost as mobile as hands, feet of Athene, feet of Joan of
Arc.

Slowly the young woman submerges once more into
the advertisements: houses for sale—she counts seventy,
that means seventy emigrants, seventy reasons for ap-
pealing to kindly Jesus. Houses wanted: two— Oh,
Kathleen ni Houlihan, what have you done to your children! Farms for sale: nine; wanted: none. Young men
who feel a vocation for monastery life—young girls who
feel a vocation for convent life . . . English hospitals
looking for nurses. Favorable terms, vacation with pay,
and once a year a free trip home.

One more look in the mirror: fresh lipstick carefully applied, eyebrows smoothed, and a dab of silver lacquer on the finger of her right hand where it had come off during the journey across the map. Once again into the passage and with the freshly lacquered fingernail one more journey to that point where the woman with the most beautiful feet in the world lives, the finger resting there for a long time, the place being recalled: six miles of steep cliffs, and on summer days the gaze into the infinity of azure, the islands floating in it as if they were figments of the imagination, islands forever surrounded by the angry white of the sea; islands that cannot be real: green, black: a mirage that hurts because it is not a mirage, because it allows of no deception—and because Aedan McNamara has to work in Birmingham so that his family can live here. Are not all the Irish on the west coast almost like tourists, because the money for their support is earned elsewhere? The azure of the distance is hard, the islands carved out of it like basalt; now and again, very rarely, a tiny black boat: people.

The roar of the surf frightens the young woman: how she sometimes—in fall, in winter, when the storms blow for weeks, the surf roars for weeks, the rain rains—longs for the dark walls of the towns. She glances at her watch again: nearly half-past one; she walks to the window, looks at the naked coin of the moon that has traveled toward the western end of the bay; suddenly the headlight cones of her husband's car: helpless as arms that find nothing to cling to, they writhe across the gray clouds, dip—the car has almost reached the top—shoot over the hill, landing first on the village roofs, dip toward the road: two more miles of bog, the village, and then the horn, three times, and again: three times, and everyone in the village knows: Mary McNamara has had a boy, punctually in the night of September 24/25; now the postmaster will jump out of bed, send off the telegrams to Birmingham, Rome, New York, and London; again the horn, for those living in the upper village: three times: Mary McNamara has had a boy.

She can hear the sound of the engine now, louder, near, the headlights throw sharp shadows of the palm fronds on the white house walls, are swallowed up in the undergrowth of the oleander, come to a stop, and in the light falling from her window the young woman can see the giant copper cauldron said to come from the Spanish Armada. With a laugh her husband holds it up so that the full light falls upon it.

"A princely fee," he says softly, and the woman closes the window, throws one more glance into the mirror, and pours two full glasses of whisky: to the most beautiful feet in the world!

11. The Dead Redskin of Duke Street

Reluctantly the Irish policeman raises his hand to stop the car. He is probably the descendant of a king or the grandson of a poet, the great-nephew of a saint; perhaps, although ostensibly the guardian of the law, he also keeps his other pistol, the illegal pistol of the freedom fighter, at home under his pillow. But never was the function he performs here the theme of one of the countless songs his mother used to sing to him in his cradle: checking the name and address on the license and the number on the registration slip—what a foolish, humiliating occupation for the descendant of a king, the grandson of a poet, the great-nephew of a saint—for the man who is fonder of his illegal pistol than of the legal one dangling on his hip.

Reluctantly, gloomily, therefore, he stops the car, the Irishman inside winds down the window, the policeman smiles, the Irishman smiles, and the official exchange of remarks can begin:

"Nice day today," said the policeman, "how are you?"

"Oh, not bad, how's yourself?"

"Could be better, but it's a nice day, isn't it?"

"Beautiful—or d'you think it's going to rain?"

The policeman solemnly looks to the east, to the north, west, and south—and the sensuous solemnity with which he turns his head, sniffing the air, conveys the re-

75

gret that there are only four points of the compass; how wonderful it must be to be able to gaze sensuously and solemnly toward sixteen points of the compass—then he turns meditatively toward the driver.

"It might still rain. You know, the day my oldest daughter had her youngest child—a dear little boy with brown hair and a pair of eyes—a pair of eyes, I'm telling you!—that day, it was three years ago, about this time of year, we also thought it was a lovely day; but in the afternoon it poured."

"Yes," said the driver, "when my daughter-in-law—the wife of my second-oldest son—when she had her first baby—a sweet little girl with fair hair and bright blue eyes, a delightful child, believe me!—that day the weather was pretty much like today."

"And the day my wife had her tooth out—rain in the morning, sunshine at noon, rain again in the evening—that's just how it was the day Katie Coughlan stabbed the priest from St. Mary's. . . ."

"Did they ever find out why she did it?"

"She stabbed him because he wouldn't give her absolution. She kept on defending herself in court by saying: 'D'you expect me to die covered with all my sins?'—and on that very day the third-youngest child of my second-oldest daughter got his first tooth, and we always celebrate teeth; yet I was prowling about Dublin in the pouring rain, looking for Katie."

"Did you find her?"

"No, she had been sitting for two hours at the police station waiting for us—but there was nobody there, we were all out looking for her."

"Did she show any remorse?"

"Not the slightest. She said: 'I assume he'll go straight to Heaven; what more does he want?' It was a terrible day too when Tom Duffy took the big chocolate rabbit to the bear in the zoo, the one he pinched from Woolworth's. Forty pounds of pure chocolate, and all the animals in the zoo got excited because the roaring of the bears drove them crazy. That day the sun was shining beautifully, the whole day—and I wanted to go to the beach with my oldest daughter's oldest girl, but instead I had to pick up Tom. He was at home in bed, sound asleep, and d'you know what the fellow said when I woke him up? Did you ever hear?"

"I don't remember."

" 'Damn it all,' he said, 'why did that marvelous chocolate rabbit have to belong to Woolworth's? You don't even let a chap sleep in peace.' Oh stupid, foolish world, where the right things always belong to the wrong people—a wonderful day, and I had to arrest silly old Tom."

"Yes," said the driver, "the day my youngest boy failed his matric was also a glorious day. . . ."

If you multiply the number of relations by their age and then multiply this result by 365, you have roughly the number of possible variations on the topic of weather. You can never be sure which is more important: Katie Coughlan's murder or the weather on that particular day; who is the alibi for what is something you can never find out: whether it was the rain for Katie or Katie for the rain is always a moot point. A stolen chocolate rabbit, an extracted tooth, an exam not passed: these events do not stand alone in the world, they are part and parcel of the history of the weather, they belong to a mysterious, infinitely complicated system of coordinates.

"It was terrible weather too," said the policeman, "the day a nun found the dead Redskin on Duke Street; there was a storm, and rain was lashing our faces when we took the poor fellow to the police station. The nun walked beside us all the way and prayed for his poor soul—the water was running into her shoes, and the wind was so fierce it lifted her heavy wet habit, and for a moment I could see she had darned her dark-brown underpants with pink wool. . . ."

"Had he been murdered?"

"The Indian? No—no one ever found out where he came from, who he belonged to, no poison was found in him nor any sign of violence on him: he was clutching his tomahawk, he was in war paint and all his war finery, and since he had to have a name—we never found out what his real name was—we called him 'Our dear red brother from the air.' 'He's an angel,' wept the nun—she wouldn't leave his side—'he must be an angel; just look at his face. . . .' "

The policeman's eyes began to shine, his face, somewhat bloated from whisky, assumed a solemn expression, and suddenly he looked quite young—"Really, I still believe he was an angel; where else could he have come from?"

"Funny thing," whispered the driver to me, "I've never heard of this Indian."

And I began to suspect that the policeman was not the grandson of a poet but a poet himself.

"A week went by before we carried him to his grave, because we were looking for someone who might have known him, but nobody knew him. The most remarkable thing of all was that the nun also suddenly disappeared. Remember, I had seen the pink darning wool on her brown underpants when the wind lifted her heavy habit—there was a terrible row, of course, when the police wanted to inspect the underpants of all the nuns in Ireland."

"Did you get to see them?"

"No," said the policeman, "we never got to see the underpants; I'm sure the nun was an angel too. You know what I really wondered about: whether they actually wear darned underpants in Heaven?"

"Why don't you ask the Archbishop?" said my Irish companion; he turned his window down still farther and held out his package of cigarettes. The policeman took a cigarette.

The little gift seemed to have reminded the policeman of his real, his tiresome earthly life; his face suddenly grew old again, bloated and gloomy, when he asked:

"By the way, can I have a look at your registration?"

The driver did not even try to pretend to look for it—none of that artificial nervousness with which we look for something we know is not there; he simply said: "Oh, I left it at home."

The policeman did not bat an eyelid. "Oh, well," he said, "I expect your face is your own."

Whether the car is his too is obviously less important, I thought, as we drove on; we drove along glorious avenues, past magnificent ruins, but I saw little of them. I was thinking of the dead Indian who had been found on Duke Street by a nun, in a storm and lashing rain: I saw them both clearly, a pair of angels—one in war paint, the other wearing brown underpants darned with pink wool; I saw them more clearly than the things I might actually have seen: the splendid avenues and the magnificent ruins. . . .

12. Gazing into the Fire

It must be fun to have your own peat ditch; Mr. O'Donovan in Dublin has one, and any number of O'Neills,
Molloys, and Dalys in Dublin have them; on free days
(and there are plenty of those) Mr. O'Donovan needs
only to get on a Number 17 or 47 bus with his spade and
drive out to his peat ditch: the fare is sixpence, he has a
few sandwiches and a flask of tea in his pocket, and he
can dig peat in his own claim; a truck or a donkey cart
will carry the peat back down to the city for him. For
his compatriot in other counties it is even easier: there
the peat grows almost into the house, and on sunny days
the bare hills, striped greenish-black, are as busy as at
harvest time; here they are gathering in what centuries
of moisture have built up between naked rocks, lakes,
and green meadows: peat, the sole natural wealth of a
country that for centuries has been robbed of its forests,
that has not always had its daily bread but almost always
its daily rain, no matter how little: a tiny cloud sailing
along on a day of brilliant sunshine and—half jokingly
—squeezed out like a sponge.

Behind every house the lumps of this brownish cake
dry in great stacks, sometimes higher than the roof, and
in this way you can be sure of one thing: fire in the fireplace, the red flame licking the dark lumps, leaving pale
ash, light, odorless, almost like cigar ash: white tip to the
black Brazil.

An open fire renders one of the least attractive (and most indispensable) objects of civilized social intercourse superfluous: the ashtray; when the time the guest has spent in the house is left behind chopped up into cigarette ends in the ashtray, and the housewife empties these malodorous dishes, the stubborn, stickyish, black-gray mess remains. It is strange that no psychologist has yet investigated the lowlands of psychology and discovered the branch of buttology, for then the housewife, in collecting the chopped-up time to throw it away, could turn the butts to her advantage and practice a little psychology: there they are, then, the half-smoked, brutally bent cigarette ends of the man who never has time and with his cigarettes struggles in vain against time to gain time—there Eros has left a dark-red border on the filter—the pipe smoker the ashes of his dependability: black, crumbled, dry—there are the frugal remains of the chain smoker, who lets the cigarette burn almost to his lips before he lights the next one; in these lowlands of psychology it would be easy to find at least a few rough indices as by-products of civilized social intercourse. How kindly a fire is, consuming every trace; only teacups remain, a few glasses, and in the fireplace the glowing heart round which from time to time the master of the house piles up fresh black lumps of peat.

And all the meaningless brochures—for refrigerators, trips to Rome, "Golden Books of Humor," automobiles, and investments—this flood that, with wrapping paper, newspapers, tickets, envelopes, is rising alarmingly, here it can be transformed directly into flame; add a few sticks of wood picked up during a walk on the beach: the remains of a brandy case, a wedge washed overboard, dried out, white and clean: hold a match to the

82

pyre and at once the flames leap up, and time, the time between five in the afternoon and midnight, is so quickly consumed by the quiet flame of the fire; voices are low; for someone to shout here he must be one of two things: sick or ridiculous. Sitting here by the fire, it is possible to play truant from Europe, while Moscow has lain in darkness for the past four hours, Berlin for two, even Dublin for half an hour: there is still a clear light over the sea, and the Atlantic persistently carries away piece by piece the Western bastion of Europe; rocks fall into the sea, soundlessly the bog streams carry the dark European soil out into the Atlantic; over the years, gently plashing, they smuggle whole fields out to the open sea, crumb by crumb.

Shivering slightly, the truants put fresh peat on the fire; pieces laid carefully in layers to light the midnight game of dominoes; the needle glides slowly across the radio panel to pick up the time, but all it catches is shreds of national anthems; slowly the light in the panel dies away, and once again the flame leaps up from the peat: there is still one layer there, one hour: four lumps of peat above the glowing heart; the daily rain comes late today, almost with a smile, falling softly into the bog, into the ocean.

The sound of the departing guests' car dwindles toward lights lying scattered in the bog, on black slopes already in deep shadow, while on the beach and over the sea it is still light; the dome of darkness moves slowly toward the horizon, then closes the last chink in the vault, but it is still not quite dark, while in the Urals it is already getting light. Europe is only as wide as a short summer night.

13. When Seamus Wants a Drink. . . .

When Seamus wants a drink he must decide on when to order his thirst: as long as there are tourists in the place (and not every place has them) he can allow his thirst some degree of license, for tourists may drink whenever they are thirsty, so that the native can confidently take his place among them at the bar, especially as he represents a folkloric element that encourages tourist trade. But after September 1, Seamus has to regulate his thirst. Closing time on weekdays is 10 P.M., and that's bad enough, for during the warm, dry days of September Seamus often works until half-past nine, sometimes longer. But on Sundays he must force himself to be thirsty either up until two in the afternoon or between six and eight in the evening. If Sunday dinner takes a long time, and thirst does not come until after two, Seamus will find his favorite pub closed and the landlord, even if Seamus knocks till he comes to the door, will be "very sorry" and not in the least inclined to risk a fine of five pounds, a trip to the county capital, and a lost day's work all for the sake of a glass of beer or a whisky. On Sundays pubs have to close between two and six, and one can never be quite sure of the local policeman; there are some people who suffer from attacks of conscientiousness after a heavy Sunday dinner and become intoxicated with adherence to the law. But Seamus has also had a heavy dinner, and his longing for a glass of beer is far from remarkable, still less sinful.

So at five minutes past two Seamus stands in the village square, thinking. In the memory of his thirsty throat, forbidden beer naturally tastes better than easily obtainable beer. Seamus considers: one way would be to get his bicycle out of the shed and pedal the six miles to the next village, the landlord in the next village being obliged to give him that which the landlord in his own village must refuse him: his beer. This abstruse drinking law has the additional embellishment that the traveler who is at least three miles from his own village may not be refused a cooling drink. Seamus is still pondering: the geographical situation is unfavorable for him—unfortunately it is not possible to choose one's place of birth—and it is Seamus' bad luck that the next pub is not three but six miles away—uncommonly bad luck for an Irishman, for six miles without a pub are a rarity. Six miles there, six miles back—twelve miles for a glass of beer, and what's more, part of the way is uphill. Seamus is not a heavy drinker; if he were he wouldn't be so long making up his mind, he would have got on his bicycle long ago and be gaily jingling the shillings in his pocket. All he wants is a beer: there was so much salt in the ham, so much pepper in the cabbage—and is it decent for a man to quench his thirst with spring water or buttermilk? He gazes at the poster hanging over his favorite pub: an enormous realistically painted glass of stout, dark as liquorice and so fresh, the bitter drink, and surmounted by white, snow-white foam being licked off by a thirsty seal. "A lovely day for a Guinness!" O Tantalus! So much salt in the ham, so much pepper in the cabbage.

Cursing, Seamus goes back into the house, gets his bike out of the shed, and angrily pedals off. O Tantalus—and the power of skillful advertising! It is a hot day, very hot, the hill is steep; Seamus has to dismount, push the bicycle, sweating and cursing: his curses do not belong to the sexual sphere like those of the wine-drinking races, his curses are those of the spirit-drinkers, more blasphemous and cerebral than sexual curses, for don't spirits contain *spiritus?* He curses the government, probably also curses the clergy, who stubbornly cling to this incomprehensible law (just as in Ireland the clergy have the last word when it comes to granting pub licenses, deciding on closing time, dances), this sweating thirsty Seamus who a few hours ago was standing so reverent, so candidly pious in church listening to the Gospel. At last he reaches the top of the hill: this is the scene of the sketch I would like to write, for this is where Seamus meets his cousin Dermot from the next village. Dermot has also had salt ham, peppery cabbage. Dermot is also not a heavy drinker, all he wants is a glass of beer to quench his thirst; he too—in the next village—has stood in front of the poster with the realistically painted glass of stout, the epicurean seal, he too stood making up his mind, finally got his bike out of the shed, pushed it up the hill, cursing, sweating—now he meets Seamus: their conversation is brief but blasphemous—then Seamus races down the hill toward Dermot's favorite pub, Dermot toward Seamus' favorite pub, and they will both do what they never intended to do: they will drink themselves into a stupor, for it wouldn't be worth coming all this way for one glass of beer, for one whisky. At some time or other on this Sunday they will push their bikes up the hill again, staggering and singing, will race down the hill at breakneck speed. Seamus and Dermot, who are not drunkards at all—or are they after all?—will be drunkards before evening.

But perhaps, while he stands thirsty in the village square after two o'clock and looks at the foam-licking seal, Seamus will decide to wait, not to get his bike out of the shed; perhaps he will decide to quench his thirst— Oh the shame of it!—with water or buttermilk, to fall onto the bed with the Sunday paper. In the oppressive afternoon heat and quiet he will drop off to sleep, suddenly wake up, look at the clock and frantically—as if pursued by the devil—rush over to the pub opposite, for it is a quarter to eight, and his thirst has only a quarter of an hour left. The landlord has already begun to call out mechanically: "Ready now, please! Ready now, please!" In haste and anger, always with one eye on the clock, Seamus will down three, four, five glasses of beer, knock back several whiskies, for the clock hand is slipping closer and closer toward the eight, and the lookout posted in front of the door has already reported that the village policeman is slowly strolling across: there are some people who on Sunday afternoons suffer from attacks of ill humor and adherence to the law.

If you find yourself in a pub shortly before eight suddenly listening to the landlord's "Time, gentlemen, please!" you can watch the influx of all those who are not drunkards but who have suddenly realized the pub is closing soon and they haven't yet done what they possibly wouldn't feel in the least like doing if it were not for this insane law: they haven't got drunk yet. At five minutes to eight the crush at the bar is tremendous; everyone is drinking to ward off the thirst that may come at ten, at eleven, or even not at all. Besides, everyone feels obliged to stand the other fellow a drink: so the landlord desperately calls upon his wife, his nieces, grandchildren, grandmother, great-grandmother and aunt, because at three minutes to eight he has to draw seven rounds: sixty pints of beer, the same number of whiskies, have still to be poured, still to be drunk. This urge to drink, to be generous, has something childish about it, it is like the furtive cigarette-smoking of those who vomit as furtively as they smoke—and the final scene, when the policeman appears at the door on the dot of eight, the final scene is pure barbarism: pale, grim seventeen-year-olds hide somewhere in the barn and fill themselves up with beer and whisky, playing the sense-less rules of the game of manhood, and the landlord—the landlord fills his pockets, heaps of pound notes, jingling silver, money, money—but the law has been kept.

Sunday is by no means over, however, it is exactly eight o'clock—early yet, and the scene acted out at two in the afternoon with Seamus and Dermot can now be repeated with a cast of any number: about quarter-past eight in the evening, up on the hill, two groups of drunks meet; in order to abide by the three-mile regula-tion they are merely switching villages, switching pubs. Many are the curses that ascend to Heaven on Sunday in this pious Catholic country on which no Roman mer-cenary ever set foot: a bit of Catholic Europe beyond the borders of the Roman Empire.

14. Mrs. D.'s Ninth Child

Mrs. D.'s ninth child is called James Patrick Pedar. The day he was born was the seventeenth birthday of Siobhan, Mrs. D.'s oldest child. Siobhan's future is already settled. She is to take over the post office, look after the switchboard, receive and transmit calls from Glasgow, London, Liverpool, sell stamps, issue receipts for registered letters, and pay out ten times as much money as is paid in: pounds from England, converted dollars from America, baby bonuses, prizes for Gaelic, pensions. Every day about one o'clock when the post office truck arrives she will melt the sealing wax over a candle and press the great seal with the Irish lyre onto the large envelope containing the most important items; she will not —as her father does—have a beer every day with the driver of the post office truck and exchange a few terse remarks which resemble the severity of a liturgy more than a friendly chat over the counter. So that's what Siobhan will be doing: from eight in the morning till two in the afternoon she will sit there in the post office, with her assistant, and again in the evening from six to ten, to look after the switchboard; she will have plenty of time to read the paper, novels, or look out over the sea with her binoculars, to bring the blue islands from a distance of twelve miles to a mile and a half, the bathers on the beach from five hundred yards to sixty: women from Dublin, fashionable and old-fashioned. But longer, much longer than the short bathing season is the dead, the quiet time: wind, rain, wind, now and again a visitor buying a fivepenny stamp for a letter to the Continent, or one sending registered letters weighing three or four ounces to cities called Munich, Cologne, or Frankfurt; who obliges her to open the fat tariff book and make complicated calculations, or has friends who compel her to decipher telegraph texts from code: "Eile geboten. Stop. Antwortet baldmöglichst." Will Siobhan ever understand what "baldmöglichst" means, a word she writes so neatly in her girl's handwriting on the telegraph form, making an *oe* out of the *ö*?

In any event, Siobhan's future seems certain, as far as anything in this world is certain; even more certain appears the fact that she will get married: she has eyes like Vivien Leigh, and in the evening a youth often sits on the post office counter, dangling his legs, and one of those laconic, almost mute flirtations is carried on which are only possible in cases of ardent passion and well-nigh pathological shyness.

"Lovely weather we're having, aren't we?"

"Yes."

Silence, fleeting exchange of glances, a smile, long silence. Siobhan is glad when the switchboard buzzes.

"Are you there? Are you there?"

A plug pulled out; a smile, a glance, silence, long silence.

"Wonderful weather, isn't it?"

"Wonderful."

Silence, a smile, the switchboard comes to the rescue again.

"This is Dukinella, Dukinella calling—yes."

Plug in. Silence. Smile with the eyes of Vivien Leigh, and the young man, his voice almost cracking this time:

"Marvelous weather, eh?"

"Yes, marvelous."

Siobhan will get married but continue to look after the switchboard, to sell stamps, to pay out money, and to press the seal with the Irish lyre into the soft sealing wax.

Perhaps one day she will suddenly rebel, when the wind blows for weeks on end, when people walking along at a slant struggle against the storm, when the rain beats down for weeks on end, the binoculars fail to bring the blue islands within sight, and in the fog the smoke of the peat fires hangs close and bitter. But whatever happens she can stay here, and this is a fabulous stroke of luck: of her eight brothers and sisters, only two will be able to stay; one brother can take over the little boarding-house, and another, if he doesn't get married, can help him out there; the boardinghouse will not support two families. The others will emigrate or be forced to look for work somewhere else in the country; but where, and how much will they earn? The few men who have steady jobs here, at the dock, fishing, digging peat, or on the beach where they sift gravel, load sand, these few men earn five to seven pounds a week; and if a man has his own peat claim, a cow, chickens, a cottage, and children to help him, he can just about make a living—but in England a laborer, if he works overtime, earns twenty to twenty-five pounds a week, and without overtime at least twelve to fifteen; this means that a young fellow, even if he spends ten pounds a week on himself, will always send from two to fifteen pounds home, and there is many a granny living here on these two pounds sent her by a son or grandson, and many a family living on the five pounds sent by the father.

One thing is certain, and that is that of Mrs. D.'s nine children five or six will have to emigrate. Will little Pedar, now being patiently rocked by his oldest brother while his mother makes fried eggs for her boardinghouse guests, fills jam pots, cuts white and brown bread, pours tea, while she bakes bread in the peat fire by placing the dough in the iron form and heaping glowing peat over the form (it is faster, by the way, and cheaper than in the electric oven)—in fourteen years, in 1970, on October 1 or April 1, will this little Pedar, aged fourteen, carrying his cardboard suitcase, hung about with medallions, supplied with a package of extra-thick sandwiches, embraced by his sobbing mother, stand at the bus stop to begin the great journey to Cleveland, Ohio, to Manchester, Liverpool, London, or Sydney, to some uncle, a cousin, a brother perhaps, who has promised to look after him and do something for him?

These farewells at Irish railway stations, at bus stops in the middle of the bog, when tears blend with raindrops and the Atlantic wind is blowing; Grandfather stands there too, he knows the canyons of Manhattan, he knows the New York waterfront, for thirty years he has been through the mill, and he quickly stuffs another pound note into the boy's pocket, the boy with the cropped hair, the runny nose, the boy who is being wept over as Jacob wept over Joseph; the bus driver cautiously sounds his horn, very cautiously—he has driven hundreds, perhaps thousands, of boys whom he has seen grow up to the station, and he knows the train does not wait and that a farewell that is over and done with is easier to bear than one which is still to come. He waves, the journey into the lonely countryside begins, the little white house in the bog, tears mixed with mucus, past the store, past the pub where Father used to drink his pint of an evening; past the school, the church, a sign of the cross, the bus driver makes one too—the bus stops; more tears, more farewells; Michael is leaving too, and Sheila; tears, tears—Irish, Polish, Armenian tears. . . .

The journey by bus and train from here to Dublin takes eight hours, and what is picked up on the way, the ones standing in the corridors of overcrowded trains with cardboard boxes, battered suitcases, or duffel bags, girls with a rosary still wound around their hands, boys with marbles still clinking in their pockets—this freight is only a small part, only a few hundred of the more than forty thousand who leave this country every year: laborers and doctors, nurses, household help, and teachers —Irish tears that will blend with Polish and Italian tears in London, Manhattan, Cleveland, Liverpool, or Sydney.

Of the eighty children at Mass on Sundays, only forty-five will still be living here in forty years; but these forty-five will have so many children that eighty children will again be kneeling in church.

So of Mrs. D.'s nine children, five or six will certainly have to emigrate. But now Pedar is being rocked by his older brother, while his mother throws lobsters for her guests into the big pot over the peat fire; while the onions are simmering in the pan and the steaming bread slowly cools on the tiled table; while the sea murmurs and Siobhan with eyes like Vivien Leigh's looks through

95

the binoculars across to the blue islands, islands on which in clear weather you can make out the little villages: houses, barns, a church whose tower has already collapsed. Not a soul is living there now, not a soul. Birds nest in parlors, seals sometimes laze on the dock of the little harbor, screeching seagulls cry like lost souls in the deserted streets. It is a birds' paradise, say those who sometimes row an English professor across, an ornithologist.

"Now I can see it," says Siobhan.

"What?" asks her mother.

"The church; it's all white, all covered with seagulls."

"You take Pedar now," says her brother, "I have to go and do the milking." Siobhan lays aside the binoculars, takes the baby, rocking him as she walks about humming. Will she go to America, become a waitress or a film star, and will Pedar sell stamps, look after the switchboard, and in twenty years look across to the deserted island with the binoculars to discover that the church has now collapsed entirely?

As yet the future, farewell and tears, have not begun for the D. family. As yet no one has packed his cardboard suitcase and presumed on the bus driver's patience in order to spin the farewell out a little, and as yet no one has even given it a thought, for here the present counts for more than the future; but this emphasis, resulting in improvisation instead of planning, will be balanced with tears.

15. A Small Contribution
to Occidental Mythology

While our boat was slowly entering the little harbor, we could make out the old man sitting on a stone bench in front of a ruin. He might have been sitting there in exactly the same way three hundred years ago; the fact that he was smoking a pipe made no difference: it required no effort to transpose the pipe, the lighter, and the Woolworth cap into the seventeenth century; the old man pulled them in his wake, as well as the movie camera which George had stowed carefully away in the bow of the boat. Hundreds of years ago ballad singers, itinerant monks, had probably landed in this harbor just as we were doing; the old man raised his cap—his hair was white, fluffy, and thick—he made our boat fast, we jumped ashore and, smiling at each other, exchanged the "lovely day"—"nice day"—"wonderful day," the highly complicated simplicity of greeting in countries where the weather is always threatened by rain gods, and as soon as we set foot on the little island it seemed as if time closed over our heads like a vortex. The greenness of these trees and meadows defies description; they throw green shadows into the Shannon, their green light seems to reach up to the sky where the clouds have gathered round the sun like patches of moss; this could be the scene of Danae and the shower of gold. There is a vault of green over the island, and the sun falls in discs of gold over meadows and trees, lying there as round as coins and as bright as coins, and sometimes a coin hops onto the back of a rabbit and drops off onto the meadow.

The old man is eighty-eight; a contemporary of Sun Yat-sen and Busoni, he was born before Rumania became what it has for years no longer been: a kingdom; he was four years old when Dickens died—and he is a year older than dynamite; all this merely to catch him in the frail net of time. The ruin he was sitting in front of had been a barn built in the beginning of our century, but fifty feet farther on there was a ruin from the sixth century; fourteen hundred years ago St. Ciaran of Clonmacnois built a church here. Without the discerning eye of the archeologist, the walls from the twentieth century are indistinguishable from those of the sixth century; there is a sheen of green over them all, scattered with golden patches of sunlight.

It was here that George wanted to try out a new color film, and the old man—one year older than dynamite—had been chosen to supply the "human interest": puffing away at his pipe, he was to be filmed on the bank of the Shannon against the setting sun, a few days later he would appear on American screens, and all the Irish in America would have tears of homesickness in their eyes and begin to sing; multiplied a million times over, shrouded in veils of green light, in the rosy glow of the setting sun, and the smoke from his pipe blue, intensely blue—that was how he was to appear.

But first tea had to be drunk, lots of tea, and the visitors had to pay tribute by telling all the news; for in spite of radio and newspapers, news from the lips of the man you shook hands with, the man you had tea with, *that's* the kind that counts. We had tea in the lounge of a

98

vacant manor house; the permanent dark-green shadow of the trees seemed to have dyed the walls green, to have drawn a green patina over the Dickensian furniture. The retired English colonel who had brought us over in his boat—with his long red hair, his pointed red beard, he looked like a mixture between Robinson Crusoe and Mephistopheles—led the conversation, and unfortunately I found it hard to understand his English, although he was kind enough to try and speak "slowly, very slowly."

At first I understood only three words in the conversation: Rommel, war, and fair, and I knew that Rommel's "fairness" during the "war" was one of the colonel's favorite topics; moreover, my attention was distracted by the old man's children, grandchildren, great-grandchildren, who looked into the room or brought tea, hot water, bread, and cakes (a little five-year-old girl came with half a cookie and placed it on the table as a token of her hospitality), and all of them, children, grandchildren, great-grandchildren, had the pointed, triangular, knowing, heart-shaped face that so often looks down on the busy world in the form of a waterspout from the towers of French cathedrals. . . .

George sat holding the camera, ready to shoot and waiting for the sunset, but that evening the sun was slow in setting, particularly slow it seemed to me, and the colonel switched from his favorite topic to another: he talked about someone called Henry who had evidently been a hero in the war in Russia; from time to time the old man looked at me in wondering surprise with his round, pale-blue eyes, and I would nod; who was I to deny this Henry, whom I did not know, the heroism with which Crusoe-Mephistopheles credited him?

99

At last the sun seemed ready to set; as required by the director, it was approaching the horizon, approaching the television devotees in America, and we walked slowly back to the bank of the Shannon. The sun was dropping fast now, and the old man quickly filled his pipe, then drew on it too hastily so that it was no longer puffing by the time the lower edge of the sun was just touching the horizon. But the old man's tobacco pouch was empty, and the sun was slipping away rapidly. How dead a smokeless pipe looks in the mouth of a peasant standing in front of the setting sun: folkloric silhouette, silver hair in the green light, rosy-hued brow. George hurriedly tore up a few cigarettes and stuffed them into the pipe bowl, pale-blue smoke came puffing out, and at this very moment the sun was half-submerged behind the gray horizon: a eucharist in dwindling glory—the pipe puffed, the camera whirred, and the silver hair shone: greetings from the beloved homeland for moist Irish eyes in America, a new type of picture postcard. "We'll dub in a nice bagpipe tune," said George.

Folklore is something like innocence: when you know you have it, you no longer have it, and the old man stood there rather sadly when the sun had gone down; a blue-gray twilight absorbed the green veils. We went over to him, tore up some more cigarettes and stuffed them in his pipe; suddenly it was cool, dampness flowed in from all sides, and the island, this tiny kingdom where the old man's family had lived for three hundred years, the island seemed to me like a great green sponge lying half in, half out of the water and soaking up dampness from below.

The fire in the hearth had gone out, burned-out peat

fell over the red lumps, and when we made our way slowly back to the little harbor the old man walked beside me and looked at me strangely; the look in his eyes embarrassed me, because—yes, because there seemed to be awe in it, and I did not find myself awe-inspiring; before I got into the boat he pressed my hand, warmly, shyly, with heartfelt emotion. "Rommel," he said softly and slowly, and in his voice was all the gravity of a myth, and "Henry," he said—and suddenly everything I had not understood before, everything that had been said about this Henry, became plain to me like a watermark that can only be seen in a certain light. I realized that this Henry was me. George jumped down beside me into the boat; he had quickly taken some shots of St. Ciaran's chapel in the dusk. George grinned when he saw my face.

I drew a breath, a long breath, in order to correct the myth; it did not seem fair toward either Rommel or Henry or history to leave things as they were—but the boat had already been cast loose, and Crusoe-Mephistopheles had started up the engine, and I called across to the island: "Rommel was not the war—and Henry wasn't a hero, far from it," but probably the old man had only understood three of the words: Rommel, Henry, and hero—and once again I shouted the single word: "No, no, no, no. . . ."

On this little island in the Shannon, where a stranger seldom sets foot, perhaps tales will be told beside darkly glowing hearths, fifty or a hundred years from now, of Rommel, of war, and of Henry. Thus it is that what we call history penetrates into remote corners of our world: not Stalingrad, not the millions murdered and killed, not the mutilated faces of European cities—war will be known by the words Rommel, fairness, and for good measure Henry, who was there in person and called out in the blue darkness "No, no, no!" from the boat as it moved off—a word so easily misunderstood and for that reason so suitable for the making of a myth. . . .

George stood beside me laughing; he too had caught a myth in his whirring camera: St. Ciaran's chapel in the dusk and the old man, white-haired, lost in thought; we could still see his thick, snow-white hair shining far off against the wall of the little harbor—a touch of silver in the ink of twilight. The little island, the kingdom, sank into the Shannon with all its errors and all its truths, and Crusoe-Mephistopheles, who was at the tiller, was smiling peacefully to himself: "Rommel," he murmured; it sounded like an incantation.

16. Not a Swan to Be Seen

The red-haired woman in the compartment was talking
quietly to the young priest, who looked up every now
and then for a few seconds from his breviary, went on
murmuring, looked up, then closed his breviary and devoted himself entirely to the conversation.

"San Francisco?" he asked.

"Yes," said the red-haired woman, "my husband has
sent us over; I'm going to see my parents-in-law, I've
never met them. I have to get out at Ballymote."

"There's plenty of time yet," said the priest in a low
voice, "plenty of time." "Really?" asked the young
woman softly. She was very tall, fat, and pale, and sat
there with her child's face like a great doll, while her
three-year-old daughter had taken the priest's breviary
and was giving an excellent imitation of his murmuring.
The young woman was already lifting a hand to punish
the little girl, but the priest held her arm back.

"Don't stop her, please," he said quietly.

It was raining; water was running down the window
panes, farmers were rowing outside across their flooded
fields to fish up their hay from the water; washing hung
on hedges, at the mercy of the rain, wet dogs barked at
the train, sheep scampered away, and the little girl was
saying her breviary, weaving into her murmurs names
which she remembered from her evening prayers: Jesus,
Holy Mary, and making room for the poor souls too.

The train stopped, a soaking wet porter passed baskets of mushrooms into the baggage car, unloaded cigarettes, the bundle of evening papers, then helped a woman standing in the rain to open her umbrella. . . .

The stationmaster looked wistfully after the slowly departing train; sometimes he must ask himself whether in reality he isn't a cemetery custodian: four trains a day: two up, two down, and sometimes a freight train ambling sadly along as if it were going to the funeral of another freight train. In Ireland the barriers at level crossings do not protect cars from trains, they protect trains from cars; they are not opened and closed toward the road, the line is blocked across the tracks; in this way the neatly painted stations look something like miniature health spas or sanatoria, the stationmasters are more like orderlies than their military-looking colleagues in other countries, who are always standing in the smoke of engines, the thundering of trains, saluting freight trains dashing by. Flowers grow around the little Irish railway stations, neat, well-tended beds, carefully pruned trees, and the stationmaster smiles into the departing train as if to say: No, no, you're not dreaming, it's really true, it's really four-forty-nine, as my clock up there shows. For the traveler is sure the train must be late: the train is punctual, but the punctuality seems deceptive; four-forty-nine is too precise a time for it to be correct in these stations. It is not the clock that is wrong, but time, which uses minute hands.

Sheep fled, cows stared, wet dogs barked, and the farmers rowed around in boats on their fields and fished up the grass in nets.

A gentle singsong flowed rhythmically from the little

girl's lips, articulated Jesus, Holy Mary, wove in the poor souls at regular intervals. The red-haired woman grew more and more anxious.

"No," said the priest softly, "there are two more stations before Ballymote."

"In California," said the young woman, "it's so warm, there's so much sunshine. Ireland seems quite strange to me. I've been gone fifteen years; I always count in dollars, I can't get used to pounds, shillings, and pence any more, and you know, Father, Ireland has got sadder."

"It's the rain," said the priest with a sigh.

"Of course, I've never been this way before," said the woman, "but in other places, years ago, before I went away; from Athlone to Galway—I've done that bit often, but it seems to me that fewer people are living there than before. It's so quiet, it makes my heart stand still. I'm afraid."

The priest said nothing and sighed.

"I'm afraid," said the woman in a low voice. "From Ballymote I have to go another twenty miles, by bus, then on foot, across the bog—I'm afraid of the water. Rain and lakes, rivers and streams and more lakes—you know, Father, Ireland seems to me to be full of holes. The washing on these hedges will never dry, the hay will float away—aren't you afraid too, Father?"

"It's just the rain," said the priest, "don't let it worry you. I know that feeling. Sometimes I'm afraid too. For two years I had a small parish, between Crossmolina and Newport, and it often used to rain for weeks, the storm would blow—nothing but the high mountains, dark green and black—do you know Nephin Beg?"

"No, I don't."

"It was not far from there. Rain, water, bog—and when someone took me to Newport or Foxford, always water—past lakes or past the sea."

The little girl closed the breviary, jumped up on the seat, put her arms round her mother's neck, and whispered: "Are we going to drown, really?"

"No, no," said her mother, but she did not seem very convinced herself; outside the rain splashed against the panes, the train plodded wearily into the darkness, crawling as if through clouds of water. The little girl listlessly ate a sandwich, the young woman smoked, the priest picked up his breviary again; now—without realizing it —he imitated the little girl, the names Jesus Christ, Holy Ghost, Mary, emerged from his murmuring, then he closed the book again. "Is California really so beautiful?" he asked.

"It's wonderful," said the woman, hunching her shoulders with a shiver.

"Ireland is beautiful too."

"Wonderful," said the woman, "really, I know it is— don't I have to get out here?"

"Yes, at the next station."

As the train entered Sligo it was still raining; kisses were exchanged under umbrellas, tears were wept under umbrellas; a taxi driver was asleep over his steering wheel, his head resting on his folded arms; I woke him up; he was one of those pleasant people who wake up with a smile.

"Where to?" he asked.

"To Drumcliff churchyard."

"But nobody lives there."

"Maybe," I said, "but I'd like to go there."

"And back?"

"Yes."

"All right."

We drove through puddles, empty streets; in the twilight I looked through an open window at a piano; the music looked as if the dust on it must be an inch thick. A barber was standing in his doorway, snipping with his scissors as if he wanted to cut off threads of rain; at the entrance to a movie a girl was putting on fresh lipstick, children with prayer books under their arms ran through the rain, an old woman shouted across the street to an old man: "Howya, Paddy?" and the old man shouted back: "I'm all right—with the help of God and His most blessed Mother."

"Are you quite sure," the driver asked me, "you really want to go to Drumcliff churchyard?"

"Quite sure," I said.

The hills round about were covered with faded ferns like the wet hair of an aging red-haired woman, two grim rocks guarded the entrance to this little bay: "Benbulbin and Knocknarea," said the driver, as if he were introducing me to two distant relations he didn't much care about.

"There," said the driver, pointing to where a church tower reared up in the mist; rooks were flying round the tower, clouds of rooks, and from a distance they looked like black snowflakes. "I think," said the driver, "you must be looking for the old battlefield."

"No," I said, "I've never heard of any battle."

"In 561," he began in a guide's mild tone of voice, "a

battle was fought here which was the only one ever fought in all the world on account of a copyright."

I shook my head as I looked at him.

"It's really true," he said; "the followers of St. Columba had copied a psalter belonging to St. Finian, and there was a battle between the followers of St. Finian and the followers of St. Columba. Three thousand dead—but the king decided the quarrel; he said: 'As the calf belongs to every cow, so the copy belongs to every book.' You're sure you don't want to see the battlefield?"

"No," I said, "I'm looking for a grave."

"Oh yes," he said. "Yeats, that's right—then I expect you want to go to Innisfree too."

"I don't know yet," I said; "wait here, please."

Rooks flew up from the old gravestones, circled cawing around the old church tower. Yeats' grave was wet, the stone was cold, and the lines which Yeats had had inscribed on his gravestone were as cold as the ice needles that had been shot at me from Swift's tomb: "Cast a cold eye on life, on death. Horseman, pass by!" I looked up; were the rooks enchanted swans? They cawed mockingly at me, fluttered around the church tower. The ferns lay flat on the surrounding hills, beaten down by the rain, rust-colored and withered. I felt cold.

"Drive on," I said to the driver.

"On to Innisfree then?"

"No," I said, "back to the station."

Rocks in the mist, the lonely church, encircled by fluttering rooks, and three thousand miles of water beyond Yeats' grave. Not a swan to be seen.

17. In a Manner of Speaking

When something happens to you in Germany, when you miss a train, break a leg, go bankrupt, we say: It couldn't have been any worse; whatever happens is always the worst. With the Irish it is almost the opposite: if you break a leg, miss a train, go bankrupt, they say: It could be worse; instead of a leg you might have broken your neck, instead of a train you might have missed Heaven, and instead of going bankrupt you might have lost your peace of mind, and going bankrupt is no reason at all for that. What happens is never the worst; on the contrary, what's worse never happens: if your revered and beloved grandmother dies, your revered and beloved grandfather might have died too; if the farm burns down but the chickens are saved, the chickens might have been burned up too, and if they do burn up—well, what's worse is that you might have died yourself, and that didn't happen. And if you should die, well, you are rid of all your troubles, for to every penitent sinner the way is open to Heaven, the goal of our laborious earthly pilgrimage—after breaking legs, missing trains, surviving all manner of bankruptcies. With us—it seems to me—when something happens our sense of humor and imagination desert us; in Ireland that is just when they come into play. To persuade someone who has broken his leg, is lying in pain or hobbling around in a plaster cast, that it might have been worse is not only comforting, it is an occupation requiring poetic talents, not to mention a touch of sadism: to paint a picture of the agonies of a fractured vertebra, to demonstrate what a dislocated shoulder would be like, or a crushed skull—the man with the broken leg hobbles off much comforted, counting himself lucky to have suffered such a minor misfortune.

Thus fate has unlimited credit, and the interest is paid willingly and submissively; if the children are in bed, racked and miserable with whooping cough, in need of devoted care, you must count yourself fortunate to be on your feet and able to look after the children. Here the imagination knows no bounds. "It could be worse" is one of the most common turns of speech, probably because only too often things are pretty bad and what's worse offers the consolation of being relative.

The twin sister of "it could be worse" is an equally common phrase: "I shouldn't worry"—and this among people who have every reason not to be *without* worry every minute of the day and night; a hundred years ago, during the great famine, with several consecutive crop failures, that great national disaster which not only had immediate devastating effects but the shock of which has been handed down through generations to this day—a hundred years ago Ireland had some seven million inhabitants, Poland probably had just as few at that time, but today Poland has more than twenty million inhabitants and Ireland scarcely four million, and Poland —God knows—has certainly not been spared by its powerful neighbors. This dwindling from seven to four million among a people with a surplus of births means a great tide of emigrants.

Parents watching their six (often eight or ten) children grow up would have reason enough to worry day and night, and no doubt they do worry, but with that submissive smile they too repeat the phrase: "I shouldn't worry." As yet they don't know, nor will they ever know exactly, how many of their children will populate the slums of Liverpool, London, New York, or Sydney—or whether they will be lucky. But one day the hour of farewell will come, for two out of six, for three out of eight: Sheila or Sean will go off to the bus stop, cardboard suitcase in hand, the bus will take them to the train, the train to the boat; floods of tears at bus stops, at railway stations, at the dock in Dublin or Cork in the wet, cheerless days of autumn—across the bog past abandoned houses, and not one of those who stay behind weeping knows for sure whether they will ever see Sean or Sheila again; it is a long way from Sydney to Dublin, from New York back here, and many do not even return home from London—they will get married, have children, send money home, who knows?

While almost all European countries fear a labor shortage, and many are already feeling it, here two out of six, three out of eight brothers and sisters know they will have to emigrate, so deep-rooted is the shock of the famine; from generation to generation the specter takes its terrible toll; at times one would like to believe that this emigration is some sort of habit, a duty they take for granted—but the economic situation really does make it necessary: when Ireland became a Free State, in 1923, it not only had almost a century of industrial development to catch up with, it had also to keep pace with new developments; there are scarcely any cities, or industry, or any market for the fish. Sean and Sheila will have to emigrate.

18. Farewell

It was hard to say good-by, just because everything seemed to point to its being necessary: our money was all gone, new money was promised but had not arrived, it had turned cold, and in the boardinghouse (the cheapest we could find in the evening paper) the floors were so sloping that we seemed to be sinking headfirst into bottomless depths; on a gently slanting roller coaster we glided through the no-man's-land between dream and memory, across Dublin threatened by the chasms around our bed, which stood in the middle of the room, the noise and the neon lights of Dorset Street surging round us; we clung to one another; the children's sighs from the beds against the wall sounded like cries for help from a shore we could not reach.

In this no-man's-land between dream and memory the entire contents of the National Museum, to which we returned every time the clerk at the post office told us our money had not arrived, became as distinct and rigid as the displays in a waxworks; as on a ghost train in an enchanted forest, we plunged headfirst into it: St. Brigid's shoe shone silvery and delicate out of the darkness, great black crosses consoled and threatened, freedom fighters in touching green uniforms, puttees and red berets, showed us their wounds, their identity papers, read farewell letters to us in childlike voices: "My dear Mary, Ireland's freedom . . ."; a thirteenth-century cauldron swam past us, a prehistoric canoe; gold jewelry smiled, Celtic clasps made of gold, copper, and silver hung like innumerable commas on an invisible washline; we floated through the gate to Trinity College, but this great gray place was uninhabited save for a pale young girl who sat weeping on the library steps, her bright green hat in her hand, waiting for her sweetheart or mourning his loss. Noise and neon lights coming up from Dorset Street rushed past us like time that at moments became history, monuments were pushed past us, or we past them: men made of bronze, solemn, holding swords, quill pens, scrolls, reins, or compasses; women with stern bosoms plucked lyres, their sweet-sad eyes looking back through the centuries; endless columns of young girls dressed in navy blue stood in rows, carrying hurling sticks, mute, serious, and we were afraid they would raise their sticks like clubs; closely surrounded, we swept on. Everything we had looked at was now looking at us: lions roared at us, gibbons leaped across our path, we were carried up the giraffe's long neck and down again, out of his dead eyes the iguana reproached us for his ugliness; the dark water of the Liffey, green and dirty, went gurgling past us, plump seagulls screamed, a lump of butter—"two hundred years old, found in the bog in Mayo"—floated past us like a lump of gold; with a smile a policeman showed us his Rainfall Book; for forty consecutive days he had written an o, a whole column of them, and the pale girl holding the green hat was still weeping on the library steps.

The waters of the Liffey turned black, carrying history out to sea like flotsam: archives with seals hanging from them like sounding leads, treaties with ornate initials, documents heavy with sealing wax, wooden swords, cardboard cannons, lyres and chairs, beds and cupboards, inkwells, mummies with their bandages loosened and, dark and flapping like palm fronds, drifting through the water; a streetcar conductor cranked out a long paper curl from his ticket-mill, and on the steps of the Bank of Ireland an old woman was sitting, counting dollar bills, and twice, three times, four times, the clerk at the post office returned and, with a sorrowful expression, said behind his wicket: "Sorry."

Innumerable candles were burning in front of the statue of Magdalene the red-haired sinner, the backbone of a shark swam past us—it looked like a windsock—swayed, the cartilage broke apart, the vertebrae rolled like napkin rings one by one into the night and disappeared; seven hundred O'Malleys marched past us, brown-haired, white-haired, red-haired, singing a hymn of praise to their clan.

We whispered words of consolation, clung together, were borne through parks and avenues, through the gorges of Connemara, the mountains of Kerry, the bogs of Mayo, for twenty, thirty miles, always afraid of coming across the dinosaur, but all we came across was the cinema standing in the middle of Connemara, the middle of Mayo, the middle of Kerry: it was built of cement, the windows smeared with thick green paint, and inside the cinema the projector buzzed like an angry captive beast, buzzed Monroe, Tracy, Lollobrigida onto the screen; on our railway of green shadows, still fearful of the dinosaur, we passed between never-ending walls, so far from the sighs of our children, came back to the sub-

urbs of Dublin, past palms, oleanders, through rhodo-
dendron woods, headfirst; the houses grew bigger and
bigger, the trees taller and taller, the gulf between us and
the sighing children broader and broader; the gardens
grew till they were so big we could no longer see the
houses, and we plunged into the delicate green of infinite
meadows. . . .

It was hard to say good-by, although in the morning,
in the clatter of daylight, the landlady's rough voice
swept up the flotsam of our dreams like rubbish, although the tok-tok-tok-tok from the passing bus startled us, sounding so deceptively like a machine gun being
fired that we thought it was a signal for a revolution, but
Dublin had no thought of revolution; it was thinking of
breakfast, of horse races, prayers, and celluloid shadows.
The rough-voiced landlady called us to breakfast, glorious tea flowed; the landlady sat with us in her dressing
gown, smoking, and told us about voices that plagued
her at night, the voice of a drowned brother calling for
her in the night, the voice of her deceased mother re-
minding her of the vows of her first Communion, the
voice of her deceased husband, warning her of
whisky—a trio of voices, heard in the dark back room,
where she spent the whole day alone with bottle, melancholy, and dressing gown.
"My psychiatrist," she said, suddenly lowering her
voice, "claims the voices come out of the bottle, but I've
told him he'd better not say anything against my voices,
for he lives off them after all. You wouldn't like," she
said in an altered tone, "you wouldn't like to buy my

house? I'll let you have it cheap." "No, thank you," I said.

"Too bad." Shaking her head, she returned to her dark back room, with bottle, melancholy, and dressing gown.

Downcast by the "Sorry" of the post office clerk, we went back to the National Museum, from there to the art gallery, descending once more to the dark crypt of the mummies which a visitor from the country compared to kippered herrings; our last pennies went on candles which quickly burned down in front of the colored pictures of saints; we walked up to Stephens Green, fed the ducks, sat in the sun, listened to Crimson Cloud's chances of winning: they were good. At noon large numbers of Dubliners emerged from Mass, spreading out into Grafton Street. Our hopes of a "Yes" from the post office clerk remained unfulfilled. His "Sorry" had become more and more depressed, and he was not far—it seemed to me—from opening the cash drawer and giving us a loan from the Postmaster General; at least his hands twitched toward the drawer, and with a sigh he replaced them on the marble counter.

Luckily the girl with the green hat invited us to tea, bought the children sweets, placed some fresh candles in front of the picture of the right saint, St. Anthony, and when we went back to the post office the clerk's smile beamed at us all the way across to the entrance. He cheerfully licked his fingers, counted the notes out onto the marble top, in triumph: once, twice, several times, he gave us the money in small bills because he en-

117

joyed counting it out so much, and the coins fell with a silvery tinkle onto the marble; the girl with the green hat smiled: hadn't she placed the candles in front of the right saint?

It was hard to say good-by; the long rows of girls dressed in navy blue, carrying hurling sticks, were not threatening now, the lions had stopped roaring, only the iguana continued to reproach us with his dead eyes for his ancient ugliness.

Jukeboxes boomed, streetcar conductors cranked out long paper clouds from their ticket-mills, steamers hooted, a light wind came from the sea, many, many barrels of beer were heaved into the dark bellies of ships, even the monuments were smiling; the darkness of the dream had been lifted from quill pen, reins, lyre, and sword, and it was only old evening papers that were floating out to sea on the Liffey.

In the new evening paper there were three letters to the editor demanding Nelson's downfall; thirty-seven houses were offered for sale, one was sought, and in a tiny place in Kerry, thanks to the activities of the local festival committee, there had been a real festival: sack races, donkey races, rowing competitions, and a slow-bicycle race, and the winner of the sack race had smiled at the press photographer; she showed us her pretty face and her bad teeth.

We spent the last hour on the sloping floor of the boardinghouse bedroom, playing cards as if we were on a roof—there were no chairs or table in the room; sitting among our suitcases, the window open, teacups beside us on the floor, we chased the knave of hearts and the ace of spades through the long rows of their kind, the cheerful noise of Dorset Street surging round us; while the landlady stayed in her back room with bottle, melancholy, and dressing gown, the chambermaid smiled as she watched us play.

"That was a nice one," said the taxi driver who took us to the station, "a delightful one."

"Who was?" I asked.

"The day," he said. "Wasn't it a beauty of a day?" I agreed; as I was paying him I looked up, along the black front of a house: a young woman was just putting an orange milk jug out onto the window sill. She smiled at me, and I smiled back.

Epilogue – Thirteen years later

In the thirteen years—a baker's dozen—that have passed since this book was written, Ireland has leaped over a century and a half and caught up with another five, and it is high time for me to close my file on Ireland, postpone my visions of writing another book about that country until some distant date in the future, and quietly allow my accumulating notes to disappear into the sewing basket. One of these notes, which crops up four times, gives me a good idea of how Ireland has changed; it is a memo headed: The Dogs of Dukinella—the first is dated 1958, the three others 1960, 1963, and 1964, but by 1965 there was no further need for me to make the same note again, for the dogs of Dukinella were no longer doing what, until 1964, they used to do at least once and often several times a day when I drove through the village to the beach: no longer do they run alongside the car, dangerously close to the bumper, a new dog from property to property, from wall to wall, each one picking up the barking of the previous one like relay runners; they don't run after any cars at all, I suppose they are used to them by now, and perhaps this tells the whole story. Long ago, because I loved their enthusiasm, their temperament, and their intelligence, I smuggled the dogs of Dukinella into a story that has nothing whatever to do with Ireland but a great deal to do with Germany. There are a number of other disturbing memos that keep coming to light: The People in the Settlement, or: Sunday Mass in Front of the Valley School; the sewing basket is full.

Thirteen years later, in an Ireland that has caught up with two centuries and leaped over another five, it would no longer occur to me to have a Red Indian drop from the sky, and Limerick is no longer the Limerick of 1954. Very well, then. Moreover, to my regret but not to that of most Irishmen, nuns have practically disappeared from the newspapers; other things have disappeared too: the safety pins and the smells, the latter again to my regret but not to that of most Irishmen, for I have not only a very good nose but a keen sense of smell, and a world without smells is less to my liking than a world where they still existed. And a certain something has now made its way to Ireland, that ominous something known as The Pill—and this something absolutely paralyzes me: the prospect that fewer children might be born in Ireland fills me with dismay. I know: it's all very well for me to talk, it's easy for me to want them in large quantities: I am neither their father nor their government, and I am not required to part from them when many, as they must, start out on the road to emigration. Nowhere in the world have I seen so many, such lovely, and such natural children, and to know that His Majesty The Pill will succeed where all the Majesties of Great Britain have failed—in reducing the number of Irish children—seems to me to be no cause for rejoicing.

During these thirteen years something much worse has happened: because I have read a great deal about Ireland, I know a certain amount, one might even say a lot, about it, yet it is not by any means enough; my innocence is a thing of the past, and still my guilt, my knowledge, are inadequate. I have also read a great deal of Irish writing, and this utterly un-uniform unity that is Ireland has spoken to me most clearly of all through its literature. Beckett, Joyce, Behan—all three are intensely, almost outrageously, Irish, yet each is far removed from the other, farther than Australia from Europe. It is almost impossible to say anything about a country in which such an extraordinary character as Parnell could flourish and be betrayed—and how he was betrayed; or Biggar, the member of Parliament who, I feel, might be called the real inventor of the theater of the absurd: by declaiming meaningless texts he brought the English Parliament to a standstill for hours, for days, at a time; a country in which another no less extraordinary character flourished: Michael Collins, the "laughing boy," who was probably also betrayed. Finally it was Irish poets who began and finished something that seemed rather touching at first but did not end touchingly; it was madness, what they did, but in its madness more realistic than what was begun by that aging intellectual called Vladimir Ilich Ulyanov. Eighteen months before Lenin took over the remains of an empire, the Irish poets were scraping away the first stone from under the pedestal of that other empire which was regarded as indestructible but has since turned out to be far from it. A monument to one of these poets, Thomas Kettle, bears the words:

> Died not for flag, nor king nor emperor,
> But for a dream, born in a herdsman's shed
> And for the secret scripture of the poor.

I have read a lot about Ireland and learned a lot about it

too, and the most important fact of all seems to me to be the one that has been "scientifically," i.e., "objectively" confirmed by observation satellites: that the Irish live closer to Heaven than anyone else in Europe: to be precise, a hundred and twenty feet. This may offer some consolation to our mother the Church, patient and stern as she is, when the discussion of His White Majesty The Pill finds its way inexorably, inexorably, into the last provincial Irish paper, while the nuns (especially the ones surrounded by from four to seven brothers and sisters) disappear from the newspapers. With irresistible force His White Majesty is not only approaching the incomparable beaches of green Erin but reaching the last cottage in the bog, far away in the west, where Connaught begins, where the donkeys, consumed with love, bray goodnight to one another.

I was driving right across Ireland from Dublin, westward to where the green waves beat on lonely white beaches, the day good Pope John lay dying; my car radio was not working, so along the way I asked for news at filling stations, tearooms, newsstands, and cigarette counters, and wherever that wonderful Irish ice cream is to be bought (an Irish world record that I have probably overlooked—the consumption of ice cream), and I found Ireland fully informed. Nowhere in the world, I am sure, did people listen so avidly, so breathlessly, to the news bulletins. Just before I got to Castlebar, in a lonely wayside inn, at about nine in the evening, I felt like a drink of that miraculous potion they brew on the banks of the Liffey, and as I entered the inn I saw there was no need for me to ask about the Pope's condition. The tears of the beer-dispensing landlady, the faces of the silently drinking men: I knew that *this* White

Majesty was dead. Again: our gracious mother the Church does not, I feel, need to worry too much about the loyalty of a country that is actually her oldest and most faithful daughter, and still faithful, Celtic, like that other, Gallic daughter who, although she persists in claiming the title for herself, is no longer as faithful as all that.

People of other countries might well misunderstand or consider illogical the fact that this most faithful daughter of the Church is the classic land of strikes: the most unlikely groups—bank employees, for example—suddenly feel inspired to push through their demands for higher salaries by going on strike, and they set about it with that dogged determination that in the final analysis is the same quality that brought victory to the Irish Rebellion. It is surely an insane situation when, in a modern country with a modern economy, checks must be accepted for weeks, for months, merely on trust; when some places—department stores, for instance—have an excess of cash that at the end of the day cannot be deposited in the bank, while others, such as automobile dealers, who work without cash, are faced with a shortage of it; it is indeed insane when a completely modern economy suddenly places itself in a position of barter and "Trust me, fellow countryman," and it is part of such illogical insanities that, in an absurd financial situation of this kind, so-called business life does not collapse. Logicians of Continental background would sagely predict a disaster, but this did not happen in Ireland; things began to get ridiculous when—the strike went on for a long time and, like most strikes in Ireland, started off during the tourist season—people suddenly began running out of checks, and traveler's checks were no longer presented to the bank, but strangely enough nothing "collapsed," the situation turned into a kind of hilarious national sport that acted like a shot in the arm to the striking bank employees. An overwhelmingly Catholic country, then, in which strikes flourish as obedience does elsewhere. One man—but that was after the third pint—told me the next thing would be a strike of priests and nuns.

The thing that really prevents me from "correcting" or "adding to" what I have written about Ireland is this: I am too attached to it, and it is not good for an author to write about a subject to which he is too attached. But of course: there have indeed been many changes, and it almost looks as if during the years 1954 and 1955 we had caught Ireland at that historic moment when it was just beginning to leap over a century and a half and catch up with another five. Perhaps I can escape from my dilemma by acknowledging at least *one* omission: the fact that the world owes yet another word to Ireland—the word "lynch." Honor and glory are due to the Irish women who bring such lovely children into the world, to the Irish tinkers, and to the fuchsia hedges—I gladly take these three rose petals, as nostalgic as they are charming, out of the sewing basket and confess my weakness for them. And finally I must mention a railway conductor on a pilgrim train, a man whom we have much to thank for. In the English-speaking world there is a magic phrase guaranteeing immediate and unqualified assistance: "stranded family," and on this particular Sunday we found ourselves in this felicitous situation when suddenly my car brakes totally and utterly failed, at the very moment when I was driving downhill toward a jolly, laughing horde of boys and girls on their way to a donkey race. In childish glee (how could they possibly

126

know that my brakes had given out!) they ran right into the path of the car, waving and shouting—and I had no alternative but to drive into the nearest Irish wall and crash the car, after calling out to the family—who a moment later became a stranded family—to take cover. Now in this unusual country, which clearly has a feeling not only for strikes but also for the Sabbath, neither trains nor buses run on Sundays, and all I could do was follow the advice of a passer-by and ask the stationmaster at Claremorris if we could travel by one of the pilgrim trains (for *they* run, needless to say!). We were given permission and shown courteously, with all our baggage, into the dining car so that all the way to Dublin we could listen over the loudspeaker to a variety of rosaries, comments, sermons, and hymns; but that wasn't what was so exceptional, nor was it so exceptional that I managed to talk the dining-car steward into letting us have a few little bottles of whisky (we had really earned it: it's not every day that one deliberately drives into a wall); what was exceptional was the skill of the conductor to whom we paid our fares: he performed four actions simultaneously—crossed himself (while telling his beads), read a newspaper, smoked, and accepted our fares all at the same time.

For someone who is Irish and a writer, there is probably much to provoke him in this country, but I am not Irish and have sufficient grounds for provocation in the country about which and in whose language I write; in fact, the Catholic provocation in the country whose language I write is enough for me.

Cologne, 1967

Heinrich Böll